The Old-Time Brand-Name Cookbook

Recipes, Illustrations, and Advice from the Early Kitchens of America's Most Trusted Food Makers

BUNNY CRUMPACKER

ABRADALE PRESS
HARRY N. ABRAMS, INC., PUBLISHERS

For Chick

e   n   t   s

*T*oday's simplest kitchen operation—breakfast, maybe, or tea and cookies in the afternoon—meant hours of work a century ago, usually by several people. There were no gas or electric stoves, no refrigerators, no canned foods, no packaged foods. Forget microwaves and supermarkets—that would have been science fiction, which also didn't exist yet.

Yesterday's Kitchen: The Early Days of Convenience Cooking

Keeping a kitchen and feeding a family was day-long work. It meant labor that had to begin long before anybody's stomach produced an empty rumble.

About the middle of the nineteenth century, the open hearth was gradually replaced by the iron stove. It burned either wood or coal—hours of work in either case. Coal had to be shoveled, and wood had to be cut and stacked; cold ashes had to be scooped out and disposed of; the fire had to be laid and started; once going, it had to be stoked and replenished; the oven temperature had to be guessed at and then maintained. When the cooking was done, the stove had to be polished to keep it presentable. And then the ashes had to be scooped out again.

In the morning, the chickens had to be fed and the eggs gathered. The cow had to be milked. The butter had to be churned from yesterday's milk. The pig had already been slaughtered and the side smoked; now the bacon had to be sliced. Only when all this had been done could the cook put on her apron and actually begin to cook.

In order to keep all this going three times a day, along with cleaning, washing, ironing, sewing, mending, and child care, most houses, even those at the lowest income levels, depended upon servants. Nearly everybody had at least one girl in the kitchen; in the South, she was usually Black, in the North and the West, a recent immigrant. Families with more money employed a maid as well as a cook. In the grandest households, there were simply dozens of servants. The ratio of waiters to guests at a formal dinner

What a comfort to have an abundant supply of luxurious hot water—all you want—at any time, for dish-washing, for bathing, and for all housekeeping needs. It can be yours with an Automatic Storage Gas Water Heater.

"The Associated Customer,"
Associated Gas and Electric, 1929

in the 1850s was supposed to be one to four, which is why there was also a butler who supervised the staff.

The single girl in the kitchen had basically the same chores as the staff in the big house on the hill. Duties were not determined by finances; dinner depended on what was available. There were no refrigerators—instead there were cold cellars and, later, ice boxes. Cookbooks offered recipes for sour milk baking as well as for fresh. There was no baking powder, no powdered gelatin, no ground coffee. White sugar was scarce, expensive, and cumbersome (it was sold in chunks, sometimes in huge cones, covered with net to keep flies away, and then hung from the ceiling to be chipped at when needed).

Canned foods, except for preserves, were new and considered potentially dangerous. Fresh vegetables and fruits were available in the summer and fall, but by winter and spring, all that was left were cabbage and potatoes and those root vegetables that could make it through the winter, kept in a cold cellar or the near-frozen soil. Pickles added bursts of flavor to a bland diet.

Farmers' wives (in the first half of the nineteenth century, 90% of the American population lived on farms) raised their own food and traded (the derivation of butter and egg money) for the few things they couldn't provide for themselves: sugar, salt, pepper, tea, coffee, flour, and such treats as raisins and chocolate. Some farmers grew their own sorghum cane, and their wives pressed it, and boiled the juice down to make molasses. In towns and cities, housewives depended on peddlers and market stalls, and the peddlers and marketers depended in turn upon erratic shipments, by boat or wagon, of meat and staples. No one ran out to the corner store for a quart of milk; instead, the milk pail was carried to the cow. In the poorer parts of cities, families bought "swill milk," from scrawny cows that had been fed on distillery wastes. Swill milk was yellowish, and sometimes the cow's owner would whiten it with chalk.

The Kitchen Revolution Begins

It was the Industrial Revolution that caused the Kitchen Revolution. There were new inventions, and then, suddenly, there were factories to manufacture them. Factory work demanded little skill and paid better than kitchen work. Certainly the hours were better. Household help became more and more scarce. But household help became less and less necessary, because of the factories. It was a paradox and a circle: The factories took the labor force away from the kitchens and the parlors, but gave back the products that replaced the labor.

By the 1840s, the new iron stove was becoming the center of kitchen work, as the hearth had been before it. It was compact, off the floor, and relatively efficient. It burned wood or coal. But the true beginning of the new era was marked by the arrival of the first gas stove in the 1850s. It was patented in 1866 but for a long time, people were afraid of it. It was to be thirty years more—a generation—before the gas stove appeared less sinister. How very devilishly easy it must have seemed, a sulfuric sort of marvel, simply to turn a handle and have a flame appear. No wonder no one trusted it! In Puritan America, where work was virtue, the gas stove seemed a product of Lucifer himself. Indeed, it did occasionally blow up.

The first electric range was exhibited in London in 1891. By 1913, it had begun to appear on the market. On the cold front, things were moving at the same pace. The cold cellar and the ice house were supplemented in about 1830 by the ice box with its huge chunk of melting ice and its drip pan, which had to be emptied every day. Some families, the more fastidious, maybe, or perhaps just those with nervous husbands, kept their ice boxes on the back porch so that the ice man wouldn't have to trek through the house. Mama had to go outside, though, fairly often.

By the early 1900s, gas refrigerators had followed the trail blazed by gas stoves into modern kitchens. The first electric refrigerator, with its important looking round top—machined art deco—was sold in 1916. It cost about $900, a truly staggering sum then—more than a new car. Two decades later, the electric refrigerator, with its tiny freezer section for "cubed ice," was affordable and indispensable.

As the population of America increased and the horizon moved west, placing farms farther from consumers, the demand for more and better preserved food accelerated, and the means followed.

The First Processed Foods

In France, Louis Pasteur learned to sterilize milk and to inoculate sheep and hogs against anthrax. In America, Gail Borden, the son of a frontiersman who became the first of many food innovators, invented a dehydrated meat biscuit. Sure it

YOU CAN PREPARE MEALS IN ADVANCE...

With your General Electric Refrigerator to aid you, you can do much of your meal preparation in advance by putting to good use those "odd moments" which occur in every household every day.... Here are some of the things you can do which will relieve that last-minute confusion at mealtime and leave you free to enjoy the company of your family and guests:

- *Make up salad dressings, put into jars.*
- *Prepare lettuce or other salad greens.*
- *Mix up a recipe for Refrigerator Rolls.*
- *Make a supply of pastry, wrap in waxed paper.*
- *Make aspic jelly and keep in jars.*
- *Make a batch of Refrigerator Cookie dough, wrap in waxed paper.*

- *Make medium thick white sauce and keep in tightly covered jar. It will be ready for creamed soups, vegetables, or for escalloped dishes.*
- *Look over the dinner menu and see what can be done in advance.*

Often as many as three meals can be prepared at one time.

"Silent Hostess Treasure Book,"
GE Refrigerators, 1930

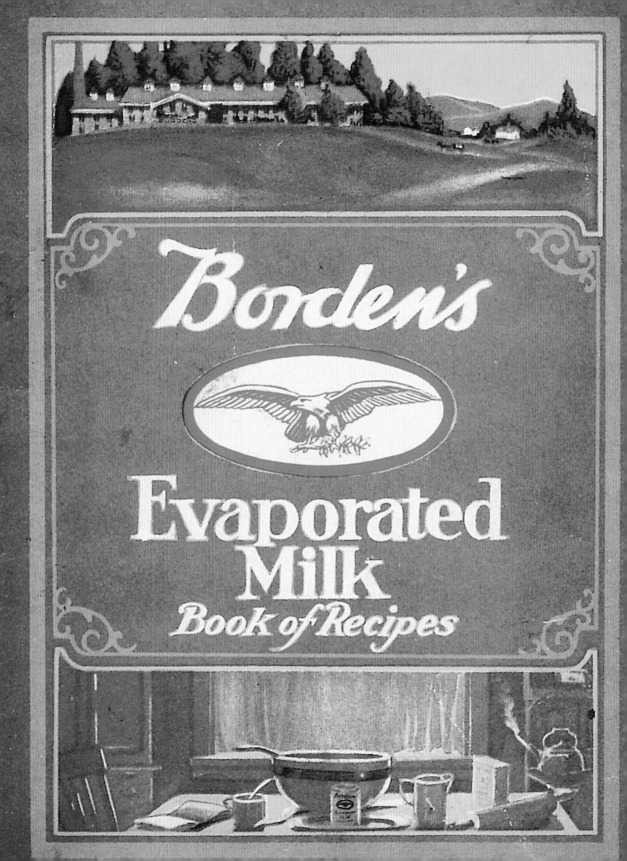

Borden's

Evaporated Milk
Book of Recipes

meant his fortune, he spent all his own money and everything he could borrow to fund a trip to London to the International Exposition of 1852. Things didn't go well, and he had to come back by steerage (perhaps eating his own biscuits). On the ship, he saw hundreds of families crowded together. He watched immigrant children, huddled in miserable spaces with their families, grow sick and die from drinking the milk of infected cows, kept on board to furnish milk, cream, and butter. Once back home, he did not forget what he had seen. Four years later, he patented a process for condensing and canning milk. This was the birth of the age of convenience food. It was no longer necessary to be personally acquainted with a cow in order to have a reliable source of milk.

No one then could have foreseen what the logical extension of Gail Borden's evaporated milk would be: hamburger extender and frozen biscuits, dehydrated marshmallows and imitation blueberries. The road to instant rice and cake mix was marked by the invention of products we no longer think of as "processed" or "convenience." It's almost as if they grew that way, perhaps in the peanut butter fields or hanging from the instant coffee trees.

From our perspective, it seems as if all these changes took place in a parade, each product going proudly by, in a series of small and inevitable steps forward.

In 1890, Charles B. Knox watched his wife making calves' foot jelly. It was a tedious process requiring hours of simmering in order for the broth to reduce enough to gel after it cooled. Perhaps Mr. Knox missed his wife's company; perhaps he minded the smell; perhaps he thought Mrs. Knox spent too much time in the kitchen; perhaps he knew a good idea when he had one.

He was a salesman. He had heard of powdered gelatin. It occurred to him to package powdered gelatin in small quantities for easy use in the home kitchen. Mrs. Knox worked out a collection of recipes to be given away with

You have no doubt noticed, while pouring the hot water on some gelatines, a sickening odor which will arise from it (this never will happen in pure gelatines), and shows that the stock is not pure, so is unfit for food.

Knox Gelatin, c. 1895

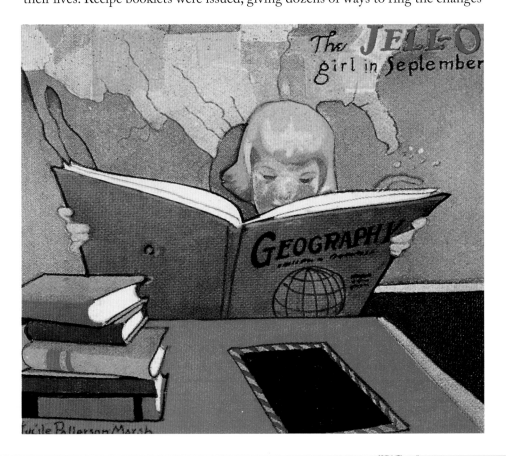

their gelatin, to show how easily it could be used with consistent and fine results. The union of taste and convenience—love and marriage—was on its way into millions of kitchens.

Jell-O came along a few years later, the next logical step. A couple in upstate New York thought of adding sugar and fruit flavoring to the gelatin. All that was needed was to convince housewives that the sweet powder in the little square box would change their lives. Recipe booklets were issued, giving dozens of ways to ring the changes

The JELL-O
girl in September

GEOGRAPHY

Lucile Patterson Marsh

The JELL-O girl in December

on Jell-O. There were recipes for desserts and salads that could be made in minutes, that would always taste the same, and that were guaranteed to be fail-safe. Jell-O, and jelled food in general, became status food: You had to be able to keep it cold. That meant you had an ice box, and that was, for a while at least, a mark of status. It sometimes seemed as if anything that could be eaten could be jelled—from the first course to the last, from soup to nuts. The Jell-O pamphlets, published by the company that bought the recipe for the sweetened powder, include recipes for soups, salads, and meat as well as endless varieties of dessert puddings. Jell-O was bought by the

Genesee Pure Food Company, and then was itself purchased by the Postum Company in that company's expansion move in the mid-1920s; Postum eventually became General Foods.

The beverage Postum was part of the process that resulted in the hundreds of varieties of breakfast cereal we are presented with today. But breakfast cereal owes something to indigestion, too.

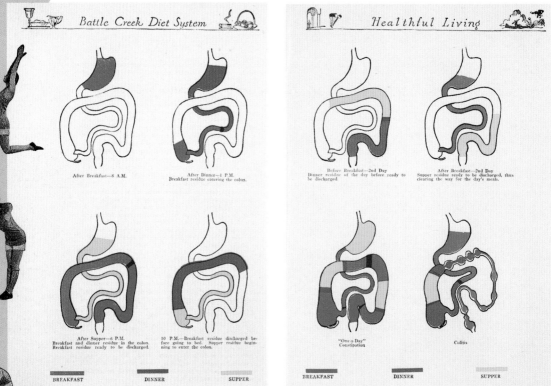

Digestive problems were rampant a hundred years ago, for many reasons: lack of refrigeration, for one; hygiene problems, for another; a heavy, greasy diet with insufficient fiber, for a third. Patent medicines were hawked from coast to coast, but they were not preventative, and frequently not really curative, either. One of the first to address the causes of all the intestinal aches and pains of the age was the Reverend Sylvester Graham—who gave us Graham crackers and Graham flour. He believed that flour caused all the trouble, and he promoted whole-grain unsifted flour as a cure-all. He was also a teetotaler and a vegetarian, and opposed to spices on the ground that they were aphrodisiacs. One of his disciples founded the Western Health Reform Institute in 1866, and a few years after that, Dr. John Harvey Kellogg was hired as manager and changed the name of the Institute to the Battle Creek Sanitarium.

Among the procedures at the Sanitarium: Patients who were underweight were fed twenty-six times a day, and between meals had to lie motionless in bed with sandbags on their stomachs on the theory that this would help their bodies

DYSPEPSIA OUR NATIONAL DISEASE

Wherever men and women are allured by the fascinations of

business life and social endeavor away from the simple and natural

life it is not an exaggeration to say that nine out of ten of them are

either sufferers from chronic indigestion or from occasional

derangements of the stomach or bowels.

Many sociologists declare, indeed, that most of our crimes may

be traced to indigestion.

"Shredded Wheat Dishes," Shredded Wheat, 1910

absorb the nutrients they needed. Physical activity of any kind was forbidden to them—they were not even allowed to brush their teeth—because moving would burn up the calories they needed so badly. Patients with high blood pressure ate grapes. Just grapes. Between ten and fourteen pounds a day. Enormous attention was given to what went into bodies, and what came out of them.

Dr. Kellogg had been influenced by another nineteenth century food faddist, Horace Fletcher, who believed that much of the digestive process took place in the mouth; therefore food should stay in the mouth as long as possible. The way to keep it there was to chew, and chew, and chew: every mouthful had to be chewed at least one-hundred times. (Liquids were to be swished around in the mouth for a minimum of thirty seconds before they were swallowed.) Kellogg gave his guests hard crackers at breakfast, and chewing them proved difficult—digestive problems were on the brink of being replaced by dental ones. Dry cereal—corn flakes—made life easier.

One of the patients at the San, as the Battle Creek Sanatorium was fondly known, was Charles W. Post. He had an ulcer, and was forbidden to drink tea or coffee. He developed a beverage made from grains, and eponymously called it Postum. He also came up with his own dry breakfast cereals, Grape-Nuts and Post Toasties. A Grape-Nuts pamphlet published by the Postum Company assures us that the "nut-like granules" offer "just enough resistance to the teeth."

And so the kitchen revolution continued, with factory-made product after product making life in the kitchen easier. In 1894, a sailor at a boardinghouse in Boston complained because the puddings served up at dinner were too lumpy. He had seen tapioca pounded in mortars in the South Seas so it would be easier to use, and he suggested that the cook grind her tapioca before cooking. The result: lump-free puddings. She began to sell ground tapioca to her neighbors. Business boomed; she called her new product "Minute Tapioca." It was the first minute food to be so designated. It added the awareness of the virtue of speed to the housewife's burgeoning convenience consciousness.

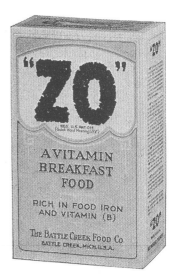

Preserving food had always been an important part of kitchen work, carrying the home through the winter, through the lean times. Salting, curing, smoking, sugaring—all of these came ages before canning and freezing. And so did pickling, in brine and in vinegar, in crocks and in barrels. Mason jars appeared in the mid-nineteenth century, and cans came later. They'd been around, but they weren't really safe. In the late 1870s, a new method of canning under steam pressure was developed; it meant reducing heating time, it was safer, and it made possible the commercial production of canned goods. It meant the housewife could now buy the pickles she'd always had to put up herself.

Henry J. Heinz began by selling pickles to groceries around Sharpsburg, Pennsylvania in 1869. His "57 Varieties" were synonymous with pickles and ketchup for years. In 1893, his display at the Chicago World's Fair was a smash hit. More than one-million people visited, tasting samples, and taking home tiny green metal Heinz pickles to add to their key chains or charm bracelets. In New York City, a six-story green pickle bearing the letters H-E-I-N-Z stood where Fifth Avenue crossed Twenty-third Street, until the Flatiron Building took the pickle's place.

In 1898, John T. Torrance, who had a Ph.D. in chemistry, figured out how to solve the problem of the large cans the manufacturers of soup needed for their products. Condensed soup was the answer, and the Joseph P. Campbell Company of Camden, New Jersey was the result, another entry on the time-line of processed food production.

> *What a difference there is between the active life of a savage and our modern living conditions. We live in a tempo of tensions. Our nerves are taut. Our minds are working under pressure all the time. We sit at a desk all day long. We spend the afternoon playing bridge. We stay indoors too much. We eat a hurried luncheon of highly refined foods which are lacking in bulk. We neglect regular toilet habits. Is there any wonder that a great majority of us suffer from constipation?*
>
> **"New Way of Living," The Kellogg Company, 1932**

Even peanut butter had to be invented. It started as a health food, developed by a doctor in St. Louis in 1890 as an easily digested high-protein product. It was a huge success—how could it not be? It wasn't just healthy; it tasted good. Grocers kept it in big tubs, stirring it up for customers before ladling it out.

Butter is man-made, though we don't usually think of it that way. Margarine is, in a manner of speaking, even more man-made than butter. It was invented in response to Napoleon III's offer of a handsome prize to whomever could find a way to produce "a cheap butter for the Army, Navy, and needy classes...." The resulting margarine (pronounced with a hard "g" in France) was made of suet mixed with milk and churned into solid fat. Later, the liquid oil—"oleine"—was

KERR SCREW BAND

KERR MASON LID
(WITH THE NATURAL GRAY SEALING
COMPOSITION FLOWED IN)

KERR MASON CAP (COMPLETE)

The Screw
Band

Kerr
Mason
Lid

separated from the lard; the solid part was called "stearin" or "margarine," and the hard fat resulting was called "butterine." Later still, the liquid oleine was hardened by hydrogenation. Solid vegetable fats like Crisco were manufactured later as marvels of hygiene; they could be kept at room temperature almost forever.

Even tea bags have a place in the processed food procession. It was just past the turn of the twentieth century when a tea merchant, Thomas Sullivan, decided to send samples of his various blends to his customers. He devised little hand-sewn bags to hold the samples. The great leap was made by his customers, who discovered that they could put a bag in a cup and pour boiling water over it. That doesn't sound like much to us, but it was the gulf between a pot and a cup, and it was large. The customers ordered more tea—but now in tea bags.

Iced tea was equally accidental. Various people had cooled their own glasses of tea over the years, but it took the St. Louis International Exposition in 1904 to make it popular. It happened, according to the story, when the man with the tea booth realized no one was buying his tea because they were already too hot—the weather was steaming, just like the tea. In desperation, he put a chunk of ice in the tea urn. His iced tea was a sensation. (The St. Louis fair also gave us the ice cream cone—when the ice cream vendor ran out of dishes and another merchant saved the day by making instant cones out of the wafer cookies *he* was selling.)

There are those who say that hamburgers were put on a bun for the first time at that same St. Louis Fair in 1904. Hamburgers trace their name back to Germany; they travelled from Russia's Baltic provinces—where chopped beef was eaten raw—to Hamburg. The raw meat (called Steak Tartare) was cooked in Hamburg and eventually emigrated to America, where it became known as hamburger. Another favorite immigrant is the hot dog, which is known as a Frankfurter in Vienna and a wiener in Frankfurt. Hot dogs derive their name from a 1906 cartoon in which the German meat inside the long bun was a wiggling dachshund. Hot dogs are made of beef, pork, mutton, goat (yes, goat), chicken, or turkey, plus fat, cereal fillers, and preservatives.

By the turn of the century, food processing was big business, accounting, by itself, for 20% of all American manufacturing. The four largest areas of the food industry—meat packing, flour milling, sugar refining, and baked goods—were either already dominated by large corporations, or soon would be.

The Kitchen Liberation of Women

In the *Boston Cooking School Cook Book*, first published in 1896, Fannie Merritt Farmer put all these achievements together for the first time and moved them yet ahead a step. She brought science to cooking. There were no more "dashes" of this or "pieces" of that—a lump of butter as big as a walnut, or a handful of raisins. Fannie Farmer insisted on level, consistent measurement, and on accurate cooking temperatures as well.

She believed that cooking was a precise art—that any dish could be reproduced in any kitchen, provided its recipe were as accurate as a scientific formula meant to be reproduced in a laboratory. It was this approach to food, coupled with advances in food preservation and preparation methods, that freed women from the hours of drudgery which had bound them to their coal stoves and wooden sinks as securely as if their apron strings had been tied around the faucets and handles as well as around their waists.

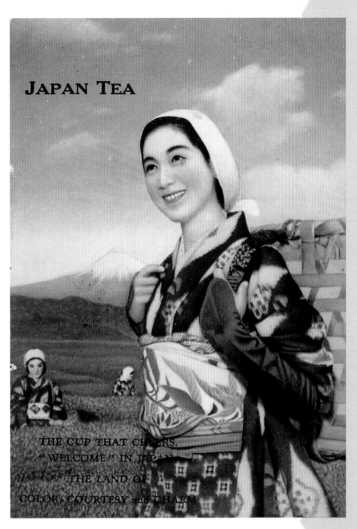

JAPAN TEA

THE CUP THAT CHEERS.
"WELCOME" IN JAPAN
THE LAND OF
COLOR, COURTESY and CHARM

Every step in the path from ice house to ice box to refrigerator to freezer, from the open hearth to the self-cleaning oven, from packaged yeast to canned peaches, was a move towards the emancipation of women from the kitchen, and toward the art of cooking as well.

The turn of the twentieth century was when all these changes bubbled at their peak, before absurdity took over from the reason of convenience foods and imitation food boomed. After World War II, artificial tastes and flavor stretchers, stabilizers, and enhancers, made madness out of good sense. Until then, each new product maintained its integrity, filled a need, tasted *real*. Even canned food didn't become widespread until it was not only safe (everyone thought it caused ptomaine poisoning) but was also of good quality. Until then, housewives preserved food by pickling, salting, and smoking it, stewing it in sugar, drying it in the sun, or fermenting it. They didn't can it until they were sure it would taste good and it wouldn't give anyone a stomach ache.

Then the advertising and merchandising began.

Something different had happened to the business of food: It had always been the selling of available food to a hungry market. Now, the consumer had to be *convinced* to buy one kind of food rather than another. Where once the food business had meant growing food, transporting it, and selling it, at the turn of the last century the food business also began to mean processing food and marketing it. What had been a question of *filling* a demand was now a matter of *creating* a demand.

How do you create a demand? By selling an idea. By persuading and convincing. By advertising.

The Recipe Pamphlets

Some of the earliest food advertisements were the pamphlets published by the new companies. Taking a cue from Mrs. Knox's collection of recipes, reams of cooking booklets were issued, all showing how many ways one food product could be used. Especially if it were the right brand.

GETTING
HIS OWN
BREAKFAST

SHREDDED WHEAT

Shredded Wheat

Ready-Cooked — Ready-to-Eat

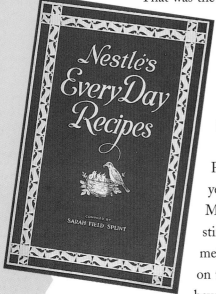

That was the idea behind the recipe pamphlets: They offered a thousand and one dishes, each using the same product, each created by an expert. They also showed the lady of the house how to use the new product—the magic powdered gelatin, the instant baking powder. They taught her how to cook, now that the kitchen maid had given notice and gone to work in the factory.

The result was to join kitchens from New York to San Francisco in a chain of Knox gelatin and Fleischmann's yeast, Rumford baking powder, Minute Tapioca, and Jell-O. Merchandising of convenience foods was the spoon that stirred the American melting pot when we still believed that melting was both possible and good. Golden Glow Salad was on the menu in Maine just as it was in Minnesota. You could have cottage pudding for dessert in Nashville or New York City. It was a pre-media nationalization of American culture.

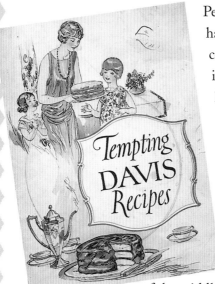

The cooking pamphlets were used with good faith. People still believed that the result of hard work was happiness. Dinner would surely please if it were cooked with the best ingredients and with care, and if the family were well fed it would be healthy and happy and grateful to the cook. A well-run kitchen, a scientific diet, and dainty food could keep you safe. No demons could enter a house where a woman knew how to make a decent white sauce; no marriage could fail if Little Mrs. Bride knew how to bake a good cake.

The pamphlets also mark a time when American kitchens were passing from the majesty of the aristocracy to the homogeneity of the middle class. Finger bowls with leaves of rose geraniums floating in them were as impractical as the white gloves ladies wore to dinner. There would soon be no one around to pluck the geranium leaf or pass the finger bowl; no one wanted to spare the time to wash the gloves, which were removed and placed in the lap as soon as everyone had seen them, anyway. Servants had other, better, work to do. It was time for madam to learn how to cook.

The recipes provided by these miniature cook books were meant for beginning cooks as well as for the experienced cook who was ready to try something new. They were easy to follow; they were

often excellent; they were always devised by experts whose purpose it was to make a single product indispensable. It was the manufacturer's dream that housewives would follow his instructions and use his brand and then buy it happily ever after. (Their sweet, pure, simple minds would, of course, be uncorrupted by visions of his competitors' products.)

My brand is safe, they each said, and reliable, and they were usually right. My brand will make you happy, they each claimed, and thus they ventured onto more metaphysical ground.

Some of these pamphlets were the only cook-books their owners possessed, and they provided recipes for everything from a loaf of bread to frozen mousse. Many of the pamphlets ended up tucked in the pages of a larger and less parochial book, Fannie Farmer, perhaps, or stuffed into drawers or desk cubbies. Some of them came with a loop of string threaded through a hole in one corner so they could be hung from a kitchen nail near the stove.

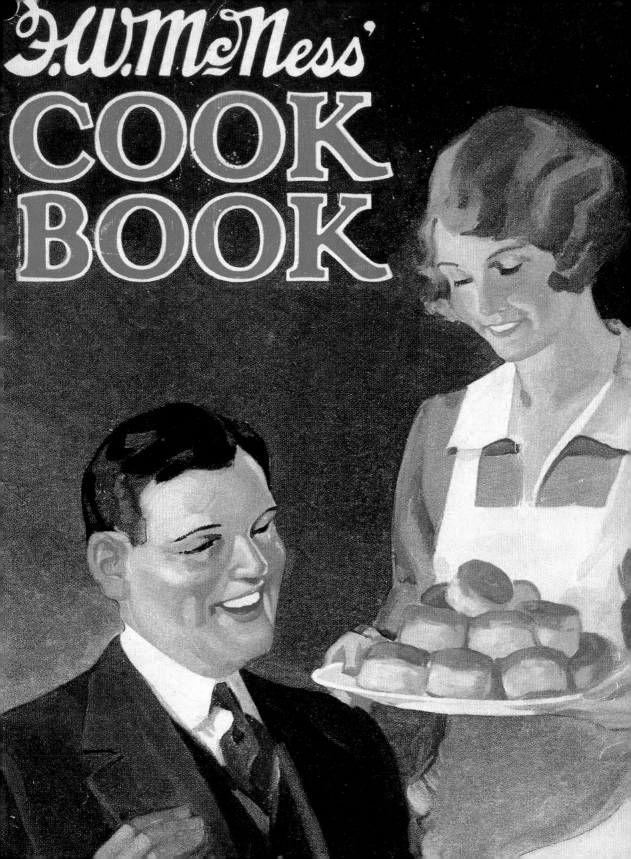

The recipes, like the booklets themselves, show a touching combination of naiveté and emerging sophistication. Every flour booklet has recipes for gems and biscuits, golden cake and sugar cookies, but there are also, popping up among the popovers, directions for making Spanish rice and Italian cream. These recipes reflect an increasing awareness of what the rest of the world eats for dinner. Wars and airplanes and television changed the American national food consciousness, but before these huge forces were in place, we were experimenting, in a timid way, with "Mexican Jelly Salad" and "Norwegian Canapés."

Food was amazingly bland in the first part of the twentieth century. These new dishes—chili con carne and "Goulasch as the Hungarian Shepherds Used to Make It"—were adventures, but they were not adventurous. The Goulash had a mere quarter-of-a-teaspoon of paprika in it.

They shall rise up and call her blessed—this woman who—loving and thoughtful of future joy and health—secures the goodness of Nature at her best, and cans against the barren sameness of the Winter months.

"Ball Blue Book," Ball Preserving, 1934

The French statesman and writer Talleyrand is supposed to have said England was a country with twenty-four religions and only one sauce. America was not very different. White sauce covered everything. It flowed from coast to coast, wherever there was a tablespoon of butter, another of flour, and a cup of milk. It was seasoned with salt and pepper. Period. Gradually, other ingredients crept in: lemon juice with fish, or a bit of cheese in a gratin. These were also the days when butter and milk and eggs and cream were good for you. Sugar, of course, was simply sweet.

Inevitably, things began to get more complicated. Exotic food began to arrive: pineapples and oranges and bananas. Recipe pamphlets introduced them, and showed us how to cook with them.

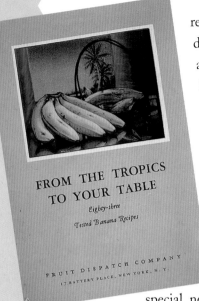

FROM THE TROPICS
TO YOUR TABLE
Eighty-three
Tested Banana Recipes

FRUIT DISPATCH COMPANY
17 BATTERY PLACE, NEW YORK, N. Y.

Manufacturers began to glamorize cooking itself. At first, recipe booklets were pamphlets for a revolution. In a way, they dealt with the common sense of the kitchen—how to cook and clean—and the rights of woman as cook. They might have been Tom Paine's, though, of course, their message was more muted. When those first battles had been won—now no one spent hours reducing beef broth to make gelatin—the merchandisers turned to face new scrimmages.

When there was no longer a need to convince women that a specific product could save them time and energy, the message changed: This product is more economical, or more nutritious, or more delicious. These are the values to be found in this package and not in that one. Knowing all this, the cook would be enveloped by a special, new kind of glow as she worked—a glow that still glimmers in food advertising today. The road from taste appeal to sex appeal is a very short one, as Adam and Eve taught us all.

Each product brought its vision of happiness into the kitchen. "They'll love you when you serve..." Even beyond this, cooking became a good deed that went past its first virtue of filling the stomach with appetizing food. Particular products could be counted on to taste better, to taste more real, to taste—even then!—more like mother's. And they had a monopoly on health. The virtuous struggle seemed always to be to get the food inside your loved ones; once there, the product could be counted on to turn into a barricade against the raging germs outside. There was no penicillin then, only chicken soup.

When all of this had succeeded—convenience, speed, domestic science, nourishment, and taste—the recipe pamphlets began to depend on glamour, for the kitchen, for the dining room, and for the woman who had made it all possible (with a little help from the secret package). It was not only that if she used the right brand she too would be glamorous. It was very much that the food itself should be part of the general striving for an ambiance of elegance and tone. Even the stars had to eat, after all. "Favorite Recipes of the Movie Stars" proved it. This booklet was much larger than most, as is only fitting, and it plugged breakfast, lunch, dinner, and the movies.

CHILI—AS IT WAS THEN

Here are two early recipes for chili. They both speak of the days when Spanish Rice was an exotic food. The first recipe has never heard of chili powder (not to mention cumin, oregano, chili peppers, or even salt and pepper). And it is to be served at an after-the-theater luncheon. Was theater then something you did BEFORE lunch? An early morning show, perhaps, followed by a bottle of catsup...

Fry a pound and a half of hamburger and one small onion, chopped, in large skillet until meat is cooked. Add a large bottle of catsup and cook until mixture appears oily. Then add a can of red kidney beans and allow to cook until mixture appears dry. Then serve.

This can be prepared and kept in the Frigidaire to be reheated when desired for serving.

It is a most acceptable Sunday night supper dish and makes a popular after-the-theater luncheon.

Six to eight servings
From "Your Frigidaire," Frigidaire, 1933

This second recipe is a little more advanced: it uses salt and pepper AND a quarter teaspoon of chili powder—IF DESIRED. The tomato comes from a can of tomato soup, instead of catsup.

Brown one pound ground beef in a skillet with one tablespoonful butter and a chopped onion. Add a medium can of Heinz Oven Baked Red Kidney Beans and stir until well blended. Pour over this a small can of Heinz Cream of Tomato Soup. Season, using one teaspoonful salt, a dash of pepper, and ¼ teaspoonful Chili Powder (if desired). Serve with boiled or baked potatoes or with boiled rice.

From "Savory Meat Dishes," Heinz, c. 1930

It may be well to remind the housewife that the Pure Food Laws of this nation do not guarantee the purity of food products. All they vouch for is that the food complies with the label outside.

**"Delicious Desserts and Candies,"
Dr. Price's Vanilla Extract,
1923**

Now the transition was complete; voyage done. The freezer was on the horizon and take-out food just down the pike. Modern women have come by their freedom in the kitchen through the cumulative effect of all these small and separate achievements. Technology in the bedroom—contraceptives—gave women a choice about how many babies to have and even when to have them. Technology in the kitchen—up to today's microwaves and frozen foods and everything we take for granted—gave women a choice about how to spend their days, now that their nights were secure.

Dinner used to grow in the garden. What couldn't be picked, plucked, or pickled was scarce and few could afford it. Today, the fortunate cook has a near infinity of ingredients from which to choose. Our kitchens are a triumph of technology, from the sleek, cool microwave to the least little no-stick frying pan.

What gets cooked in that kitchen is equally up-to-date: foods such as pre-cooked rice, pre-sliced carrots, pre-soaked beans, pre-shredded cole slaw.

The market place has become equally marvelous. Everything (from packaged salads to eighteen varieties of mustard) is all in one place, every day, and always the same.

But now we've learned not to be satisfied, even with mashed potato flakes and soup in microwavable cardboard cups. Everything

Partially Ripe Banana with green tip—The starch is not yet fully converted into sugar; in this condition bananas should not be eaten raw, but may be cooked in many tempting ways as a vegetable or a dessert.

Yellow Ripe Banana—All green color has disappeared and the pulp contains only a very small percentage of starch. The fruit now has a delicious flavor and can be readily digested by any healthy person.

Fully Ripe Banana flecked with brown—The banana is now at its best for flavor and nutrition. It may be eaten freely by everyone.

continues to simplify, concentrate, dehydrate, and—maybe—improve. The spin is to make everything faster and easier. There's only a small distance between tonight's dinner and the dinner of the future—a take-out little green pill?—but there's a vast space between shopping, cooking, and eating today and the kitchen of a hundred years ago.

Our great-grandparents ate by the calendar: strawberries in June, raspberries in July, tomatoes in August, apples in the fall, and jam in the winter. When they slaughtered a pig, they ate fresh meat. The rest of the time, there was salt pork. Life pivoted (as it always had) on the need to guarantee that there would be food for dinner. We've come so far from those days of necessary self-sufficiency, when each house had its own fruit trees, butter churn, vegetable garden, chicken coop, and cows in the barn, that living off the land, no longer a necessity, is now a fashion.

The cooking pamphlets are a reminder of what was. They're filled with simplicity and a kind of sweet innocence. They're full of hope and trust. Our present is their future. Their recipes are the flavors of our food heritage, a kitchen history of our family tree. These are our kitchen treasures. 🐐

*T*he majority of recipes included herein were selected by internationally famous food experts from the returns of a world-wide contest in which 121,619 housewives, here and abroad, competed.

"A Cook's Tour," Minute Tapioca, 1929

Starters, Soups, and Salads

Bermuda Relish Canapés

O ne of the canapés that made James Beard famous, when he began in the food business as a caterer, was his onion sandwich: rounds of thin slices of onion sandwiched, with mayonnaise, between rounds of brioche, the edges slathered with mayonnaise and then rolled in chopped parsley. These innocent Bermuda Relish bits must be kin, like a cousin once-removed, from a generation or so earlier. In other words, they got there first. They're oniony, but the end result is not as sharp as you might expect. The sweeter and milder the onion, of course, the sweeter and milder the Bermuda Relish. Try Vidalias, in season (they're really barely onions at all) or red onions—and even those benighted souls who don't love onions will find these canapés hard to resist.

6 slices of white bread, crusts removed (Use a good bread or, even better, a small brioche, a brioche loaf, or challah)
1 to 2 tablespoons sweet butter, at room temperature

¼ pound cream cheese, at room temperature
6 thin slices of red or Vidalia onion, quartered

1. Toast the bread on one side and spread the untoasted side lightly with butter.
2. Spread half the cream cheese over the buttered side. Quarter each slice.
3. Top each toast quarter with a quartered onion slice.
4. Spread the remaining cream cheese over the onion slices. (It helps to hold the onion down with one finger.)
5. Just before serving, preheat the oven to 350 degrees. Bake the toasts on a cookie sheet until the cheese is slightly browned, about 10 minutes.

Note: If you feel strongly that butter *and* cream cheese is just too much fat, leave out the butter.

Serves 6 to 8

Adapted from "Cheese Recipes"
Baumert Cheese, c. 1925-1935

Cheese Canapés

For years, cookbooks often included a recipe that called for a mixture of cream cheese, blue cheese, butter, and Cognac, to spread on crackers. We actually used to eat that way! (And it was delicious.) This recipe, which dates to the 1920s, may be that rich combination's antecedent. It leaves out the butter, and cuts the richness of the cheese with a bit of tomato. The pamphlet version calls for sherry, but I prefer to include as a choice, in honor of the cheese and crackers I once enjoyed, the same old Cognac.

¼ pound cream cheese (about ½ cup—
    half of an 8-ounce package)
3 tablespoons Roquefort cheese
½ teaspoon Worcestershire sauce
1 teaspoon Cognac, Sherry, or milk
¼ teaspoon sweet paprika
6 slices of good white bread, crusts removed
12 thin slices of tomato

1. Blend the cream cheese with the Roquefort. (A food processor is the fastest way to do this.)
2. Add the Worcestershire, Cognac, and paprika, and blend well.
3. Cut the bread in quarters or rounds. Toast on one side.
4. Spread the untoasted sides with the cheese mixture, and top each with a slice of tomato. (If you have cut the bread into quarters, do the same with the tomatoes.)

Serves 6 to 8

Adapted from "Cheese Recipes"
Baumert Cheese, c. 1925-1935

Florida Spread

When George Washington was a lad—19 years old, in 1752—he traveled to Barbados with his brother, Lawrence, who had been told he needed to recover from a recent illness in a warm climate. George sampled the native fruits. He wrote about grapefruit, called Shaddock after the English sea captain who had brought the seeds from Polynesia, and his personal favorite, pineapple ("none pleases my taste as do's the pine"), and the fruit he noted as especially abundant and most popular among the locals, the "agovado."

Agovados—otherwise known as avocados—traveled to Florida in 1833 when a local horticulturist planted the Mexican variety on his land south of Miami. The century was to change yet again before avocados became commercially successful in the early 1900s.

This recipe was proudly published in 1933 to spotlight the wonders of the modern refrigerator. The pamphlet notes that it should be "served extremely cold as you may so easily do by chilling it in your Westinghouse refrigerator for an hour."

1 avocado, peeled
1 cup crab meat, picked over to remove
   cartilage and filaments
pinch of salt
freshly ground black pepper to taste

SOUR CREAM DRESSING:
   ½ cup sour cream
   1 teaspoon vinegar
   ¼ teaspoon salt
   2 teaspoons lemon juice
   dash of cayenne pepper

1. Mash the avocado (leaving it a bit lumpy) and mix with the crab meat, salt, and pepper.
2. Combine the ingredients for the sour cream dressing and stir the dressing, gently but thoroughly, into the avocado mixture. Chill. Serve as a spread for crackers or bread, or as a dip for vegetables.

Serves 4 to 6

Adapted from "The Refrigerator Book"
Westinghouse, 1933

Ginger Toasts

James Kraft came to the United States from Canada in 1904. He used some of his small savings to buy a horse and a wagon; with his remaining capital of $65, he started a cheese delivery service. Five years later, he founded J. L. Kraft Bros. in partnership with his accountant and his brothers; together they invested $15,000. The first year, Kraft lost $3,000 plus his horse. He persevered, introduced new pasteurizing processes and packaged cheeses, and, as we all know, eventually prospered. Along the way, he bought the Phenix Cheese Company, producer of Philadelphia brand cream cheese. This company was founded by farmers to replace the Empire cheese plant after that factory burned down. "Phenix" was supposed to be "phoenix," the bird that rises triumphantly from ashes to live again, but the farmers spelled it wrong. No matter. Kraft Philadelphia brand *is* cream cheese. That's triumph.

Butter that fails to come after the customary amount of churning will be hastened by a teaspoonful of The Great Arm & Hammer Soda.

"Book of Valuable Recipes"
Arm & Hammer, 1915

8 ounces cream cheese, at room temperature   2 tablespoons minced candied ginger

1. Blend the cream cheese and the ginger until smooth. (If necessary, add a bit of milk to make the mixture smooth and creamy.)

Yield: just over 1/2 cup

Note: This is especially good made ahead (and refrigerated); the ginger almost melts into the cream cheese. Feel free to add more ginger if you like, but don't overwhelm the cream cheese or your guests. It makes a lovely spread for toast or crackers, and it's awfully good with tea. It can be garnished, if you like, with chopped toasted almonds or walnuts.

Adapted from "The Refrigerator Book"
Westinghouse, 1933

Toast with Olive Oil and Cheese

*T*his recipe is from a pamphlet that features dishes from "World Famous Chefs of the United States, Canada, and Europe," with photographs and biographical notes for each. ("Jules Dauviller, chef de cuisine at the Palace Hotel, was formerly the $10,000 a year dictator of the cuisine [*sic*] in the home of Mr. and Mrs. Harry Payne Whitney in New York. The Whitneys got him from the Grand Hotel in Paris." Yes, that's correct, he was the *dictator* of the cuisine. And they paid him.)

The chefs worked in hotels from Cape May to Dresden, and they volunteered an equally wide range of recipes. Frozen pineapple with kirschwasser, Salade Ecossaise ("Choose six nice celery roots..."), Caviar Romanoff, pickled walnuts, and Maiden's Blush Appetizer (toast topped with lobster salad, caviar in a scooped-out hard boiled egg, and sliced pimento) are just a tiny sampling.

Toast with Olive Oil and Cheese is very much like what we would now call bruschetta—slices of Italian bread brushed with garlic and olive oil and baked with a variety of toppings.

4 slices of Italian bread

1 tablespoon extra-virgin olive oil

¼ cup Parmesan cheese (use a type such
    as Parmigiano-Reggiano, and grate it yourself)

freshly ground black pepper

lemon juice

1. Preheat the oven to 350 degrees.
2. Brush each slice of bread generously with olive oil. Sprinkle with the cheese, a few grinds of black pepper, and a few drops of lemon juice. Place on a baking sheet.
3. Bake until the cheese melts and the bread is lightly browned, about 5 minutes. Serve immediately.

Note: If you'd like a garlicky flavor, toast the bread lightly first, rub each slice with a halved clove of garlic, and then continue.

The mystery chef who contributed this recipe (his signature is illegible) suggests an alternative: mash anchovies with an equal quantity of butter, add chopped parsley and spread over lightly toasted bread in a thin layer. Other possible toppings: chopped tomatoes, onion, and basil marinated in a garlicky vinaigrette; chopped mushrooms mixed with minced onion, a bit of mashed garlic, oil and vinegar; or chopped olives, minced garlic and chopped parsley mixed with oil and vinegar. Use good Italian bread.

Adapted from "Ultra Select Dishes
for Afternoon Teas"
International Publishing Co., 1913

Wakimoli

Y ou probably thought guacamole came from Mexico! In "Favorite Recipes of the Movie Stars," published in 1931, Helen Twelvetrees called this recipe Wakimoli, which makes it sound as if it came from Hawaii.

Ms. Twelvetrees (whose real name was Helen Jurgens) starred in a series of tear-filled movies in the late twenties and the thirties, but her recipe is quite joyful. It has the blandness of the food of her time, but here, the blandness—no chili powder, no garlic, no lime juice, and of course, no cilantro—is a kind of blessing, because what you end up with is a very intense avocado flavor. It's delicious. And it's kept fresh and green by the mayonnaise, even more lavish in the original recipe, which called for a full cup.

2 ripe avocados
½ small onion, chopped fine
¼ cup mayonnaise plus
    1 tablespoon (regular or low fat)
salt and freshly ground black
    pepper to taste
pinch of sweet paprika
garnish (optional): a sprinkle of
    chili powder

1. Scoop out the avocados and mash (use a fork or a food processor) until only a bit lumpy.
2. Add the onion, ¼ cup of mayonnaise, and seasonings.
3. Pile the Wakimoli into a glass serving dish—the color is so pale and pretty!—and spread a thin layer of mayonnaise, using the additional tablespoon, across the top to ensure that it will stay green.

Note: Serve as a spread with crackers or corn chips, use to stuff endive leaves, spread on bread and add thinly sliced onions for a wonderful sandwich, or pile in the center of a salad plate and surround with sliced tomatoes, onions and black olives. If you'd like a small reminder of authenticity and roots, sprinkle with a bit of chili powder.

Yield: about one cup

Adapted from "Favorite Recipes of the Movie Stars," 1931

Cream of Onion Soup

When you think of onion soup, inevitably you think of French onion soup—onion slices simmered in a rich beef broth, topped with sliced French bread and blanketed liberally with cheese, and then baked until the cheese and bread are crusty.

This onion soup is different. It won't replace the other—why should it?—but it stands wonderfully well on its own. It's a *comforting* kind of soup, and that's a very special quality. It has a rich, nutritious flavor, naturally sweet from the onions and the milk. I think it should stand in the first rank of comfort food.

The other onion soup, a late night favorite at the old French market, is actually Polish. It was brought to the court of Louis XV by the king's father-in-law, the deposed King Stanislaus of Poland. He also invented *baba au rhum*, the sweet, spongy cake soaked in rum syrup.

Cream of Onion Soup is not as sophisticated or as continental as French/Polish Onion Soup. It's simple, honest, and good, and that's plenty.

2 medium onions, chopped	½ teaspoon salt
2 tablespoons butter	3 cups milk (fresh whole or skim, or
1 cup chicken or vegetable broth	evaporated whole or skim diluted in
2 tablespoons rice	an equal amount of water)

1. Cook the onions in the butter until they are translucent. (Don't let them brown. They should be soft and golden.)
2. Add the broth, rice, and salt and cook for 15 minutes, or until the rice is tender.
3. Add the milk, bring back to the simmer, and taste to see if additional salt is needed.

Serves 4

Adapted from "Rice—200 Delightful Ways to Serve It"
Southern Rice Industry, 1935

Cold Mushroom Soup

*T*his is an unusual and subtle jellied soup, cooling on a hot day. The relatively new electric refrigerators were hitting their stride in the 1930s—with their tiny freezer sections for ice cubes, and their Art Deco coils on top—and a jellied soup, once so difficult and time-consuming to prepare, was a mark of luxury and glamour. Be sure the seasonings are sufficient for a cold soup; you may want to add a bit of lemon juice while the broth is hot to point up the flavor.

4 teaspoons unflavored gelatin
¼ cup plus 1½ cups water
¾ pound mushrooms, cleaned and sliced
1½ cups chicken broth (homemade or low sodium)
3 thick slices of onion

1 stalk celery with top
salt and freshly ground black pepper
garnish: a sprig of parsley or watercress, or a dollop of sour cream or yogurt

1. Sprinkle the gelatin over the ¼ cup of water and let it sit for about 5 minutes. (Use a heat-proof cup.)
2. Place the mushrooms in a medium saucepan. Add the remaining 1½ cups of water, all of the chicken broth, the onion, celery, and salt and pepper to taste. Bring to a boil, lower the heat, and cook over gentle heat for 20 minutes. Strain, pressing on the solids to extract as much liquid as possible.
3. Dissolve the gelatin by placing it, in its cup, in a saucepan. Add enough hot water to the saucepan to come up the side of the cup just to the level of the gelatin. Place the pan over low heat, and stir the gelatin, which will begin to dissolve. When it has completely dissolved, stir it into the mushroom broth. Taste for seasoning and adjust as necessary. Refrigerate for at least 2 hours.
4. Garnish with a sprig of parsley or watercress, or a dollop of sour cream or yogurt.

Serves 4 to 6

Adapted from "The Silent Hostess Treasure Book"
GE Refrigerators, 1930

Hamburg Vegetable Soup

Think hamburger, and you picture that meaty circle on a bun, symbol of the hungry American at home and abroad. One theory traces hamburger's heritage back to Russia's Baltic provinces, where there was a taste for raw beef, finely chopped and well seasoned. From there, what we now call Steak Tartare migrated across the Baltic Sea to the German port of Hamburg, where eventually and inevitably, some enterprising cook tried cooking the raw meat. It was only a question of time before Hamburg steak, née Steak Tartare, crossed the Atlantic, met its destiny inside a soft roll, and was named for the home it had left behind, like many immigrants.

A marvelous use for the well-traveled hamburger meat (in 1934 still called Hamburg) is this rich and surprising soup. It tastes as if it had been simmering all day instead of just for an hour. It's both robust and very easy to make—and fast, because it's based on hamburger instead of soup meat and a marrow bone. Use good chopped meat—sirloin, round, or the packaged additive-free chopped meat; there will be less fat, and the soup will taste even better.

1 tablespoon butter	2 cups potatoes, cubed (it isn't
1 medium onion, chopped	necessary to peel the potatoes, but
2 medium carrots, diced	do scrub them)
½ cup diced celery (2 or 3 stalks)	½ cup rice or barley
¾ pound ground beef—sirloin or	1 cup peas, fresh or frozen
low fat	salt and freshly ground black pepper
1½ quarts water	to taste
2 cups canned tomatoes, crushed or	garnish: chopped parsley
chopped	

1. Melt the butter in a soup pot and sauté the onion for about 5 minutes. Add the carrots and celery and continue to cook over low heat, stirring occasionally, until the onion is soft and translucent.
2. Add the meat and, using a wooden spoon to break it apart, cook until it is no longer red.
3. Add the water, tomatoes (with their juice), and the potatoes. If using barley, add it now.
4. Bring the soup to a boil, lower the heat, and simmer for 30 minutes.
5. If using rice, add it now and continue to simmer for another 15 to 30 minutes.
6. About 10 minutes before you plan to serve the soup, add the peas and salt and pepper to taste. If fat has pooled on the surface, skim off as much as you can. Serve hot, garnished with chopped parsley.

Serves 6

Adapted from "Meat Selection and Preparation"
Armour Meat, 1934

Hindu Soup

No doubt the Minute Tapioca Company called this soup "Hindu" because it contains curry powder, though an almost infinitesimal quarter-teaspoon was in the original 1928 recipe. Curry powder was still exotic then, and American food was still quite bland.

Tapioca was exotic too, once. Its more widespread use was part of the kitchen revolution that accompanied the industrial revolution, though a bit later. Around the turn of the century, a sailor brought back to a Boston boardinghouse tales of South Sea natives pounding tapioca (derived from the tropical cassava plant) in mortars to make it easier to use. He told the cook to put her tapioca through a coffee grinder so it wouldn't lump; she did, it worked, and she started selling it to her neighbors. Soon she was calling her product "Minute Tapioca." It was the first packaged food to add the virtue of speed to that of convenience.

This soup has all those virtues: it's exotic (well, a little), it's convenient, and it's quickly made. And it's delicious.

1 small onion, chopped
1 tart apple (such as Granny Smith), peeled, cored, and chopped
1 tablespoon butter
½ teaspoon dry mustard
1 teaspoon curry powder
½ teaspoon sugar

2 cups canned tomatoes, crushed
4 cups chicken or vegetable broth
3 tablespoons Minute Tapioca
salt and freshly ground black pepper to taste (the broth may already be salted; taste carefully)

1. Cook the onion and apple in the butter until the onion is soft and translucent. Stir in the mustard, curry powder, and sugar, and continue to cook for 2 or 3 minutes. Add the tomatoes and simmer for 20 minutes.

2. Add the broth and bring to a boil. Lower the heat and stir in the tapioca. Cook, stirring frequently for 15 minutes or until the tapioca is clear. Season to taste.

Serves 6

Adapted from "From Soup to Dessert"
Minute Tapioca, 1928

Navy Bean Soup

The 1945 edition of "The Cook Book of the Stars," published by WFBL, a CBS network radio station in Syracuse, New York, was published in wartime; its cover is red, white, and blue. Many CBS radio stars—singers, comedians, journalists, actors—contributed recipes to the pamphlet. Each recipe is really a double plug: one for the radio program and one for its sponsor. In those days, programs were presented by one advertiser, and stars were very much identified with their sponsor's product.

"The First Line," sponsored by Wrigley's Gum, is one of the programs featured in the pamphlet. Its star, though, wasn't a radio personality. "This series of exciting half-hour programs," reads the pamphlet copy, "has one hero, the United States Navy.... Prepared in close cooperation with the Navy, this series brings to the nation a new understanding of the magnitude and achievements of the Navy, a surging pride in the men of the naval service, and a firm confidence in the high quality of Navy leadership."

Maybe they chose Navy Bean Soup to represent the Navy just because they loved it. On the other hand, it isn't called Army Bean Soup.

1½ cups dried navy beans
water for soaking
1 smoked ham bone (see Note)
2 carrots, diced
2 stalks celery, diced
1 medium onion, diced
2 tablespoons chopped parsley

½ teaspoon thyme
6 cups water
½ cup half and half, whole milk, or
    undiluted evaporated skim milk
¾ teaspoon sugar
salt and freshly ground black pepper
    to taste

1. Rinse the beans, discarding small pebbles. Soak overnight in water that covers them by 3 inches, or bring the beans and water to a boil, simmer for 2 minutes, remove from the heat, and let stand for 1 hour. Drain.
2. Place the drained beans in a soup pot and add the ham bone, vegetables, parsley, thyme, and the 6 cups of water. Bring to a boil, reduce the heat, and let simmer until the beans are soft, about 2 hours.
3. Force the beans through a sieve, or purée in a food processor. Add the half and half, sugar, and salt and pepper. Heat gently until hot, stirring often.

Note: The pamphlet notes that you may substitute 4 strips of bacon for the ham bone. The soup is also delicious without any meat at all.

Serves 6

Adapted from "The Cook Book of the Stars"
WFBL, Columbia Broadcasting System Network, 1945

Peanut Butter Cream Soup

"**P**eanut Butter," says "Helpful Suggestions," a pamphlet published by J. W. Beardsley's Sons in 1927, "has in recent years been raised to a place of prominence in the list of foods. It contains a very large percentage of protein, vitamines and fat, and is not only a favorite with children, but is easy of digestion and assimilation. It is considered an almost perfect food."

Yes. There's more protein in peanuts, by weight, than there is in steak. They're high in the B vitamins, especially niacin and thiamin, and they're a good source of phosphorous. They're inexpensive, portable, and stay fresh for a remarkably long time. And they smoosh into peanut butter.

All of this makes Peanut Butter Cream Soup rather special. It does have a high fat content (once definitely an asset), but it's mostly unsaturated. With a salad, bread, and fruit for dessert, it makes a satisfying meal.

In the original Beardsley recipe, everything was steeped in the milk, which was then strained and stirred into a butter-flour roux. I think it's more satisfying this way. Use creamy or chunky peanut butter, but chunky has a single great advantage: all those chunks. I like that texture in the final dish.

2 tablespoons butter
1 small onion, chopped
3 stalks celery, chopped
½ teaspoon paprika
2 tablespoons flour

4 cups milk
1 bay leaf
salt and freshly ground black
   pepper to taste
½ cup peanut butter

1. Melt the butter in a saucepan and sauté the onions and celery until they are soft and the onions are translucent. Add the paprika and flour, and cook, stirring, for 3 minutes.
2. Whisk in the milk and stir well, scraping up any bits on the bottom of the pan. Add the bay leaf and cook over low heat for 10 minutes, stirring often.
3. Stir in the peanut butter. It melts into the soup as you stir. Season to taste, remove the bay leaf, and serve.

Serves 4

Adapted from "Beardsley's Helpful Suggestions"
J. W. Beardsley's Sons, 1927

Tomato Soup

*I*n 1893, the United States Supreme Court established, for trade purposes, that tomatoes could be classified as a vegetable, even though tomatoes are really a fruit. I wonder how we would feel about tomatoes if we thought of them as fruits. Would our taste for them fried, baked, stewed, in sandwiches, sauces, and soups remain the same?

Tomato soup is an old stand-by. Making it this way—with a white sauce—gives it a solid, satisfying, old-fashioned taste. White sauce covered the country once, oozing from coast to coast. When it was ubiquitous, it must have been tiresome. Today, just once in a while, it's rich and savory. Use a whisk and you won't have lumps.

The pamphlet instructs the cook to strain the tomatoes before adding them to the white sauce. Puréeing them in a food processor updates the procedure and gives the soup a lovely texture.

4 tablespoons butter
3 tablespoons flour
1 cup evaporated milk
½ cup plus ¾ cup water
salt and freshly ground black
    pepper to taste

2 cups canned tomatoes
1 thick slice onion
1 stalk celery, with leaves
1 teaspoon sugar
½ teaspoon salt
⅛ teaspoon sweet paprika

1. Melt the butter in a saucepan. Stir in the flour and cook for 3 minutes, stirring frequently. Whisk in the milk and ½ cup water and cook, whisking, until thickened. Season with salt and pepper.

2. In a separate pan, cook the tomatoes, ¾ cup water, onion, celery, sugar, and seasonings for 20 minutes, stirring from time to time. Process in small batches.

3. Slowly whisk the tomato mixture into the white sauce. Heat gently until hot. Taste for seasoning and adjust if necessary.

Serves 6

Adapted from "Ten Cooking Tests"
Borden's, 1927

Beet Aspic

*T*omato aspic may be old-fashioned, but beet aspic is up-to-date. It's a beautiful deep scarlet color—it glistens. Show off its color in a glass bowl, if you have one. It's much easier to spoon aspic from a bowl than it is to unmold and slice it, though when this pamphlet was published, that would have been unthinkable.

The pamphlet calls for using fresh beets, but if you do, you'll lose the beautiful scarlet color so easily achieved by using the liquid from the canned beets. Beet aspic goes very nicely with pork or fish—the taste is much like that of pickled beets.

1 15-ounce can beets, whole, chunked, sliced, or julienned—reserve the liquid
1½ tablespoons unflavored gelatin
¼ cup water
½ cup white vinegar
½ cup sugar

1 bay leaf
½ teaspoon mustard seed
½ teaspoon celery seed
salt and freshly ground black pepper to taste

1. Place the beets in a glass serving bowl.
2. Sprinkle the gelatin over the water in a small container and let sit for 5 minutes, until it is softened.
3. Place ¾ cup of the reserved beet liquid (add water if you don't have enough) in a saucepan, and add the vinegar, sugar, bay leaf, mustard seed, celery seed, and salt and pepper. Heat until the sugar is dissolved. Add the gelatin and stir until it is completely dissolved.
4. Let the mixture cool until it's safe to pour over the beets in the glass bowl. Remove and discard the bay leaf. Place the aspic in the refrigerator for 4 hours or until set.

Serves 6

Adapted from "New Salads"
Colman's Mustard, 1928

Brewster Asparagus Salad

*I*n 1927, the makers of Premier Pure Food Products (canned foods) published a collection of recipes that, they wrote, "have been coming to us for years." It wasn't easy, they noted, to decide which recipes to include. "We wish that it were possible to publish every one," they said. "Of course, that would be an expensive undertaking and would take a very long time." They chose the recipes they considered most unusual. Miss Carrie E. Owen, who is credited with the recipe for Brewster Salad, was a resident of Shamokin, Pennsylvania. In a perfect world, she would have lived in Brewster.

1 hard-cooked egg white, chopped

1 tablespoon India relish

1 tablespoon finely chopped parsley

2 tablespoons chopped canned pimiento or
   freshly roasted red peppers

salt and freshly ground black pepper to taste

2 tablespoons mayonnaise, or a vinaigrette
   made with 2 tablespoons salad oil and
   1 tablespoon wine vinegar

1 pound fresh asparagus, cooked and cooled,
   or 1 15-ounce can of asparagus

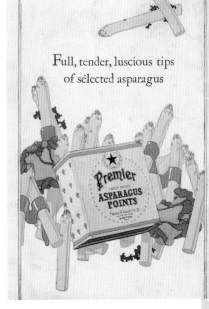

Full, tender, luscious tips
of selected asparagus

1. Mix egg white, relish, parsley, pimento, and salt and pepper. Stir in the mayonnaise.
2. Place the asparagus on a serving dish and criss-cross it with lines of the dressing.

Serves 4

Adapted from "Aladdin's Lamp at Mealtimes"
Premier Pure Food Products, 1927

Golden Wax Bean Salad

OLNEY'S PURE FOOD BOY

PICKED THIS MORNING

Trade Mark
Reg. U. S. Pat. Off.

THE TRADE MARK OF QUALITY

ABSOLUTELY PURE

THE BURT OLNEY CANNING CO.,
ONEIDA, N. Y., U. S. A.

A letter to "The Housekeeper" is featured at the beginning of the Burt Olney Canning Company's 1909 pamphlet. "Dear Madam," it begins, "Few women appreciate the possibilities of canned goods." That's partly because in 1909, canned goods were still not yet always totally safe. But the pamphlet is filled with reassurances, and sweetness, and clarity. I would trust a can of Burt Olney's beans. On the other hand, the company seems to blame the very housewives it's trying to persuade. "(Women) use (canned goods) under protest and serve them with an apology. If this is true in your case, it is because you buy indiscriminately and serve what you buy in the old stereotyped way." The letter goes on to reassure us that Olney's canned goods satisfy the government's requirements for purity; and "they will satisfy you as to flavor."

This waxed bean salad can be made with fresh beans. It can also be made—without apology!—with canned beans. Just don't buy your beans indiscriminately. And if you get tired of waxed beans, you can make the same deliciously stereotyped salad with green beans—or, for that matter, almost any vegetable from asparagus to zucchini.

1 15-ounce can wax beans, drained, or 1 pound fresh beans, cooked and cooled
2 tablespoons red wine vinegar
4 tablespoons olive oil

2 tablespoons minced onion
1 small clove garlic, minced or crushed
1 to 2 tablespoons chopped parsley
freshly ground black pepper to taste

1. Combine the beans with the remaining ingredients. (Unless you buy low-sodium beans, they will already be salted, so taste carefully before adding more.)
2. Let stand for about an hour before serving to give the flavors a chance to meld.

Serves 4

Adapted from "Soups, Salads, and Desserts"
The Burt Olney Canning Co., 1909

Russian Salad

*I*n Russia, Russian Salad is called Salade Olivier. That's its formal name, and it is a formal salad. It was supposedly devised by a French chef named Olivier, employed by Czar Nicholas II at the Winter Palace. Come the revolution, Nicholas didn't fare too well, but Olivier escaped and made his way to Berlin, where he opened a restaurant. He probably served a wicked salad.

Salads that are called "Russian" usually have caviar in them. The most elegant way to serve this salad is in a pyramid shape or a mound with a dollop of caviar on the top, but it's fine without the caviar, too. I've had it in Russian restaurants served very simply in a bowl.

Exact quantities don't matter for this flexible salad, and neither do you have to use precisely these vegetables, though the salad almost always includes potatoes.

3 cups cooked vegetables, cubed—any or all of these: carrots, cauliflower, peas, celery, string beans, potatoes, beets, asparagus
1 cup cubed cooked chicken or ham (or a combination)
¼ cup dill pickle, cubed

½ cup mayonnaise or as much as is needed to coat the vegetables
salt and freshly ground black pepper
optional: chopped dill
garnish: tomatoes, cucumber, hard boiled eggs, black olives, sprigs of dill

1. Combine the vegetables, meat, pickle, and mayonnaise and mix well. Add the seasonings and adjust to taste as neccessary. Refrigerate until ready to serve.
2. Serve on lettuce leaves, garnished as you prefer—for example, with dill sprigs and tomato, cucumber, hard boiled egg wedges, and black olives.

Note: You may wish to marinate the vegetables in a vinaigrette dressing made with olive oil and wine vinegar. In that case, be sure they're well drained before mixing the salad with the mayonnaise.

Serves 6

Adapted from "The Sunday American Cook Book"
The Boston Sunday American, 1911

Perfection Salad

*I*t isn't perfect. It's cole slaw—sort of—and it goes back to the beginnings of powdered gelatin (one of the first of the industrial revolution's processed foods). Perfection Salad, wildly popular once, was part of two trends. The first was to make gelatin molds out of everything, even cole slaw, because using gelatin was newly easy and had status: You had to be able to provide the chill, and that meant you had an ice box. The second trend was to keep food neat and clean— "dainty" was the word—dainty on the plate, and prepared by the little woman, as opposed to the big chunky maid.

In that tradition, Perfection Salad was devised by Mrs. John E. Cooke of New Castle, Pennsylvania, who entered her recipe in a contest sponsored by Charles Knox in 1905. One of the judges was Fannie Farmer. Mrs. Cooke (felicitous name!) won third prize, a sewing machine.

The thing is, Perfection Salad is good. I'm not a fan of molded food unmolded— it always seems an unnecessary bother to me, fuss for the sake of fuss—but this is a lovely looking gelatin, and if you're willing to go through the process of unmolding, you will be very well rewarded. The original recipe, in an undated Knox pamphlet, suggests cutting the salad into cubes and serving it in cases made of the shells of red or green peppers. I wouldn't go that far—using pepper shells—but I do like the idea of letting the salad jell in a square baking dish, and then cubing it, and piling the cubes on a serving dish.

And if it isn't perfect—well, what is? Perfection Salad turns out to be, at least, very good.

> Boil three or four onions in a pint of water and apply with a soft brush to gilt frames and flies will keep off them.
>
> "Guide to Health," Household Instructor, and Family Prize Cook Book, 1898

2 tablespoons unflavored gelatin
½ cup cold water
½ cup boiling water
¼ cup sugar
½ cup white or cider vinegar
2 tablespoons lemon juice

½ teaspoon salt
1 cup finely shredded cabbage
1 cup finely chopped or sliced celery
¼ cup chopped red bell pepper
freshly ground black pepper to taste

1. Sprinkle the gelatin over the cold water and let it sit for about 5 minutes until softened. Add the boiling water, sugar, vinegar, lemon juice and salt and stir until the gelatin is dissolved. Refrigerate.

2. When this mixture has begun to thicken and is syrupy, add the cabbage, celery, red pepper, and ground black pepper. Taste for salt and add more if necessary. Pour into a mold or bowl. (If the salad is to be served unmolded, rinse the mold with cold water and pour the mixture into the wet mold. A square baking dish can also be used and should also be rinsed and left wet.) Refrigerate for several hours.

3. Either serve from the bowl or unmold it by dipping the mold quickly into hot water, covering it with a serving dish, and in one fast motion, reversing so that the dish is on the bottom. Give it a firm shake and remove the mold. If it doesn't unmold, either dip it again in hot water or wrap the mold for a minute in a dish towel that has been dipped in hot water and quickly wrung out, and then try again. To serve cubes, dip the baking dish quickly into hot water. Cut the cubes with a sharp knife, run the knife around the sides to loosen them, and remove the cubes with a spatula.

Serves 6

Adapted from "Food Economy"
Knox Gelatin, c. 1905

Potato and Pimiento Salad

I love potato salad, and I like picnics a lot too. They go awfully well together, but then, potato salad goes with most things, anytime, anywhere.

Even love. Potatoes were once considered potent aphrodisiacs. "Eating of these roots doth excite Venus and increaseth lust," wrote one seventeenth-century writer. As luck would have it, many foods have been thought to be aphrodisiacs at one time or another, by one people or another. Pimientos have. So have eggs. This recipe includes potatoes, pimientos, and eggs, making, just possibly, for a nice, lusty salad. Of course, it's really not so much what you're eating as whom you're eating it with. My advice: Take a lover on a picnic and have some potato salad. After all, if nothing else, at least you'll have had a good meal. Together.

More advice, given to me once at a platonic Fourth of July picnic, and I pass it on here: The best potato salads have hard boiled eggs in them. That's the secret.

6 large boiling potatoes, scrubbed

2 canned pimientos, cubed, or 1 red pepper, cubed

4 tablespoons vegetable oil

2 tablespoons cider vinegar

2 tablespoons minced parsley

2 tablespoons minced onion

2 hard-boiled eggs, chopped

salt and freshly ground black pepper

4 tablespoons mayonnaise

1. Put the potatoes in a pot, cover them with lightly salted water, bring to a boil, and cook until tender when pierced with a knife. Drain. If you have an electric range, put the pot back on the hot burner until the remaining moisture has evaporated. Otherwise, put a folded towel over the potatoes, cover, and let sit for a few minutes—the towel will absorb the moisture.

2. While the potatoes are still warm, slice them. (Peeled or unpeeled is up to you. Sometimes, I partially peel them so the salad won't taste too strongly of peel.) Place them in a large bowl. Add the oil and vinegar, stir gently, and let stand for one hour. Stir in the remaining ingredients.

3. Taste to adjust the seasonings. You might want to add more onion, salt, pepper, or mayonnaise. Keep refrigerated until ready to serve.

The best cook will fail to furnish us with an acceptable dish if we have no appetite; but with a good appetite, any dish is welcome. "Hunger is the cook's best friend."

"Ayer's Preserve Book," Ayer's, 1898

Serves 6

Adapted from "Every Day Cooking for the Housekeeper and Student"
Rumford Baking Powder, c. 1885

Bread is toasted to extract the moisture and make it more palatable and digestible.

To make toast, use stale bread, or dry slices in oven before toasting. Cut bread thin, about one-quarter of an inch, have fire red, not blazing. The crusts may be removed or not, according to

taste. Use double broiler, place slices in evenly, close broiler and hold firmly to prevent slices from slipping. Move gently over fire one or two minutes, turn over, then hold nearer to coals and brown. Serve at once, buttered or dry.

Bread properly toasted turns the dough into pure wheat farina, easily digested even by sick persons.

Always toast over coals or in oven.

"65 Delicious Dishes," Fleischmann's Yeast, 1919

Cinnamon Toast

Cinnamon goes way back. The first written mention of it was in a paper ascribed to a Chinese Emperor in 2700 B.C. For a long time, only small amounts of cinnamon reached Europe from the East, and it remained expensive, literally worth its weight in gold.

Today, we use cinnamon liberally, in dozens of ways, from mom's apple pie to the dusting on the top of a cup of cappuccino. Of all the things we can do with a little jar of cinnamon, one of the simplest—and most appealing, if we forget how humble it is—is cinnamon toast. Cinnamon toast is often associated with childhood, and it *is* full of innocence and purity. It is also sophisticated in its way, and incredibly dependable, always easily conjured up when the last cookie is gone. It's one of those things—so quiet, so honorable, so trustworthy, such a good sport—that we often forget it's there. Our loss. Cinnamon Toast is good.

6 slices white bread	⅓ cup sugar
¼ cup butter, at room temperature	1 tablespoon cinnamon

1. Preheat the broiler.
2. In the broiler, toast the bread on one side, watching carefully to be sure it doesn't scorch.
3. Cream the butter and the sugar; mix in the cinnamon.
4. Spread the butter mixture on the *untoasted* side of each bread slice.
5. Place the slices on a cookie sheet and broil until the mixture melts and the bread is bubbly and brown. Serve immediately.

Note: Use firm white bread—Pepperidge Farm or Arnold, or a home-baked loaf. If you have an unsliced loaf, slice the pieces about ⅓-inch thick.

Serves 6

Adapted from "Bread: The Most Important of All Foods"
Spaulding's Blue Ribbon Bread, 1925

Gary Cooper's Mother's Buttermilk Griddle Cakes

Many of Gary Cooper's films (from *Sergeant York* to *High Noon*) are American classics. Griddle cakes are classic, too (pancakes cooked on a griddle = griddle cakes), and they have an ancient pedigree. Making a batter of grain and water and pouring it onto a hot rock to bake—in the sun, or near a fire—must have been one of the earliest cooking endeavors.

The first American griddle cakes were made with cornmeal. Gary Cooper's mother's griddle cakes are in that honorable tradition. It's hard to find out much about her but if this is what she made for breakfast, she was a woman of merit.

2 cups flour	½ teaspoon salt
2 tablespoons cornmeal	2 cups buttermilk
2 tablespoons sugar	½ cup milk or cream
1 teaspoon baking soda	2 eggs, beaten
2 teaspoons baking powder	2 tablespoons unsalted butter, melted

1. Set a griddle over medium heat.
2. Mix the dry ingredients in a bowl. Separately, mix the remaining ingredients. Add the liquid mixture to the dry mixture. Stir lightly with a fork—the batter should be lumpy.
3. When the griddle is hot enough—a drop of cold water will skitter across the surface and rapidly evaporate—lightly butter it if necessary and make the first pancake (the first batch is the pan's, so make only one.) Cook until bubbles cover the uncooked top surface, then flip and continue to cook for about two minutes longer. After the first pancake is done, ladle out as many as will easily fit on your griddle—usually four at a time poured from a quarter-cup measure.

Yield: 24 pancakes; serves 4 to 6

Adapted from "Favorite Recipes of the Movie Stars," 1931

Banana Waffles

Until relatively recently on the kitchen time line, bananas were fairly exotic imports. They've been around—in the global sense—for over a thousand years, but they didn't arrive in America until about 1804—and that was just one small boat load, a schooner, actually, from Cuba. A quarter of

> *AFTER ALL, Bread and milk give us all the types of material needed by the human body in less expensive form than most other foods. Therefore the more we can plan to extend expensive foods by the addition of bread and milk, the better.*
>
> **"Good Things to Eat," Fleischmann's Yeast, 1912**

a century later, another boat arrived with more bananas on board. That's how long it took. And about twenty-five years after *that*, the Boston Fruit Company wrapped individual bananas in foil and sold them at ten cents each—a high price, but they were an exotic fruit—at the 1876 Philadelphia Centennial Exposition. It wasn't until 1899 that Boston Fruit merged with United Fruit and began shipping bananas regularly to American markets. Even so, by mid-century, bananas were still exotic enough so that Chiquita Banana had to tell us never to put bananas in the re-frig-er-a-tor. ("I'm Chiquita Banana and I've come to say/Bananas must be eaten in a certain way....")

Waffles, on the other hand, came to America with the Pilgrims. They spent time in Holland before they sailed for America in 1620; the word waffle comes from the Dutch *wafel*. Thomas Jefferson, who brought recipes for ice cream and macaroni back from France, among other things, also tucked a long-handled waffle iron into his baggage. We have electric waffle irons now; the only problem is remembering which shelf we stored them on—or under. Dust it off and try these. They're exotic. And good.

1 cup flour	½ cup milk or cream
2 teaspoons baking powder	2 tablespoons butter, melted
¼ teaspoon salt	1 cup mashed bananas
3 eggs, separated	(about 2 large bananas)

1. Heat the waffle iron.
2. Mix the dry ingredients in a bowl. Add the egg yolks and milk and beat thoroughly. Stir in the melted butter and mashed bananas.
3. In a separate bowl with clean beaters, beat the egg whites until they are stiff but not dry; fold into the batter.
4. Bake in the hot iron according to the manufacturer's directions.

Yield: 12 4-inch square waffles

Adapted from "Bananas in the Modern Manner"
Banana Growers Association, 1930

Butterscotch Curls

utterscotch is a wonderful flavor: butter and brown sugar combined to make something greater than the sum of its parts. It's something like mixing two primary colors and creating Crayola heaven.

These Curls—biscuit dough curled around butter and brown sugar—are simple and fast to make. They have the old-fashioned innocence that is the hallmark of so many of the pamphlet recipes. And they're lovely at breakfast.

butter for the muffin tins

2 cups flour

4 teaspoons baking powder

½ teaspoon salt

4 tablespoons unsalted butter plus 2 to 3 tablespoons, at room temperature, for the filling

⅔ cup milk

⅓ to ½ cup brown sugar

1. Preheat the oven to 375 degrees. Lightly butter muffin tins.
2. In a food processor, mix the flour, baking powder, and salt. Pulse in the 4 tablespoons of butter until the mixture is the consistency of cornmeal. (Or, in a bowl, cut in the butter with two knives or a pastry cutter.) Add the milk and mix for a few seconds longer. The mixture will be very crumbly. It should hold together when it's pressed; if it doesn't, add an additional tablespoon of milk. Turn the dough out onto a lightly floured surface.
3. Push the dough together and knead it slightly. Roll out to a thickness of ¼ inch.
4. Spread the remaining butter over the dough. Sprinkle with the brown sugar.
5. Roll the dough up like a jelly roll. Cut across into 1-inch slices.
6. Place the slices in the muffin tins—either standing up or flat across the bottom. Bake for 30 minutes. These are best warm.

Yield: two dozen slices

Adapted from "Royal Cook Book"
Standard Brands Incorporated, 1930

Edward R. Murrow's Oatmeal Scones

*D*uring World War II, Edward R. Murrow was the quintessential foreign correspondent. He was the voice of London, broadcasting while bombs fell, bringing the immediacy of the war into millions of American homes. As Chief of CBS European Correspondents, his calm and convincing voice had special resonance. "This is London," was his tag line, and it was heard over the radio on Sunday afternoons all across America. He made the transition from radio news to television, and during the McCarthy years, he became a beacon of moral journalism.

These are his Oatmeal Scones, from "The Cook Book of the Stars," a pamphlet published by radio station WFBL during World War II.

---

²⁄₃ cup milk

1 cup cooked oatmeal

½ teaspoon salt

2 tablespoons melted unsalted
   butter

1½ cups flour (use more if dough is
   too sticky)

4 teaspoons baking powder

2 tablespoons honey

---

1. Preheat the oven to 375 degrees.
2. Mix the milk into the cooked oatmeal, and add the salt and melted butter.
3. Add the flour and baking powder. Mix well, and add the honey. If the dough seems very sticky at this point, add more flour.
4. On a well-floured board, roll the dough into a circle ½-inch thick. Cut into wedges with a floured knife, or use a biscuit cutter or an upside-down glass to cut into circles.
5. Bake for 20 to 30 minutes, or until browned.

Note: If you have any scones left over, they reheat very nicely. They also make a surprisingly good base for blueberry shortcake: gently heat a cup or so of blueberries with a quarter-cup of sugar and a tiny bit of water. Layer the shortcakes: bottom half of a scone, warm blueberry sauce, top half, whipped cream, fresh blueberries. Yum.

Yield: 12 2½-inch circle scones

From "The Cook Book of the Stars"
WFBL, Columbia Broadcasting System Network, 1945

French Muffins

Before there was baking powder, bakers often beat their ingredients by hand for at least half an hour to make them light. In the 1850s, self-rising flour—containing baking powder—was developed. Finally, in 1865, an Indiana pharmacist mixed baking soda with cream of tartar, an alkaline and an acid that react to each other when combined with a liquid by forming a gas. In a batter, they make tiny bubbles, helping the batter rise and keeping it light as it bakes. In 1867, James A. Church introduced the term baking soda (the alkaline in baking powder) to replace sodium bicarbonate, or "saleratus," an American coinage based on the Latin *sal*, salt, and *aeratus*, aerated. Double-acting baking powder came next—the bubbles begin when the baking powder and liquid meet, and finish in the oven, when the heat sets the batter around the bubbles. (That's why ovens should be pre-heated, so that the first batch of bubbles aren't lost before the heat makes them expand and captures them.)

Muffins are the next question. We all know they're little cakes—but not as sweet as cupcakes. In England, muffins are tea cakes. In America, English muffins aren't muffins. French muffins, on the other hand, are definitely muffins—and sweet morsels they are.

butter for the muffin tins	3 tablespoons unsalted butter, melted
1½ cups flour	1 egg, beaten
½ teaspoon salt	½ cup honey
2 teaspoons baking powder	1 cup milk

1. Preheat the oven to 375 degrees, and butter the muffin tins.
2. In a mixing bowl, combine the flour, salt, and baking powder. Add the butter, egg, honey, and milk, and stir to make a soft batter.
3. Place 1 tablespoon of batter in each muffin cup. Bake for 20 minutes.

Yield: 12 muffins

From "Making Biscuits"
Royal Baking Powder, 1924

Date and Nut Bread

Date palms grow in the desert—wherever there's water for their feet, as in an oasis, and hot, dry sunshine for their fruit. There were wild dates growing 50,000 years ago. Marco Polo drank date wine in India; the Egyptians, Greeks, and Romans ate dates; Muslims break the fasts of Ramadan by eating dates. The California date industry began in the early years of the twentieth century. Today we can buy dates pitted, stuffed, and even chopped, and in California, I'm told, you can buy date milk shakes. And we bake date and nut bread. When Chock Full O' Nuts was a chain of shops that sold hot dogs and good coffee, one of their most popular offerings was a date-nut bread sandwich with cream cheese. This loaf isn't as dark and dense as that kind of date-nut bread; it's light in color and texture, but it would still be lovely with cream cheese. Or with coffee, for that matter. Try toasting it, too.

butter for the loaf pan
3 cups flour
3 teaspoons baking powder
1 teaspoon salt
½ cup sugar

1 teaspoon cinnamon
¾ cup broken walnuts
1 cup chopped dates
1½ cup milk
1 egg, well beaten

1. Preheat the oven to 350 degrees, and butter a 9x5x3-inch loaf pan.
2. In a mixing bowl, combine the flour, baking powder, salt, sugar, and cinnamon. Stir in the walnuts and dates.
3. Put the milk in a cup or bowl, add the egg and beat lightly. Pour the milk mixture into the flour mixture and beat well.
4. Pour the batter into the loaf pan and let stand for 30 minutes. Bake for one hour, until a toothpick poked into the bread comes out clean. Cool on a rack.

Yield: one loaf

Adapted from "One Hundred Delights,"
Dromedary Products, 1922

Golden Corn Bread

Because the English used the word "corn" to mean any major cereal crop, that's what they called the grain they found in North America in 1608. Gradually, because this new grain was so associated with the Native Americans, English settlers began to refer to it as "Indian corn." They developed their own Indian corn dishes, like corn bread, based on recipes they learned from Native Americans. Boiled and buttered corn (or even better, poached and buttered) didn't reach American tables until about the middle of the 1800s (and didn't enter the language as an accepted term—'corn-on-the-cob'—until about 1876). Today, corn is grown for animal feed, corn meal, corn syrup, corn starch, corn flakes, and canned corn as well as for plain old corn-on-the-cob. Corn has become a major American crop, equal to the *combined* crops of wheat, oats, barley, rice, rye, and sorghum.

Adventures in Corn Meal Cookery!

I've had trouble finding a corn bread recipe I loved and could live with—one I could make on the spur of the moment, when I might not have buttermilk in the refrigerator, one that is moist and rich instead of dry and crumbly. This one, from a Quaker Corn Meal pamphlet, is what I've been looking for.

1 cup yellow corn meal
1 cup flour
¼ cup sugar
½ teaspoon of salt
3 teaspoons baking powder

1 cup milk
1 egg
¼ cup melted butter, plus butter for the baking pan

HOW TO CARE FOR BREAD

Good bread comes wrapped in a moisture-proof and dust-proof wrapper, which protects it from all foreign odors or flavors.

The wrapper should not be removed until the bread is wanted, then open one end of the wrapper, slide out the bread, and return the unused portion of the loaf.

The bread box should be scalded and aired a least once a week, and should be kept in a dry place.

SLICED BREAD

Sliced Bread offers you the added convenience of bread that is already sliced and ready to serve. No waiting—no knives to bother with—no cut fingers— no uneven slices—no crumbs—no waste. Every slice is uniformly perfect.

HOW TO TOAST BREAD

When toasting under a gas flame, light the oven at least five minutes before making the toast. Spread on the bread and toast quickly, as long toasting dries out the bread.

For buttered toast, have the butter creamed or softened so it will spread easily and quickly. Serve as soon as the toast is made.

"How I Use Taystee Bread," Taystee Bread, 1933

1. Preheat the oven to 400 degrees, and butter an 8-inch square baking dish.
2. Mix the corn meal, flour, sugar, salt, and baking powder.
3. Put the milk in a cup or bowl, add the egg, and beat lightly. Add the melted butter and beat again. Pour the milk mixture into the flour mixture and combine, beating for about a minute. Don't overbeat.
4. Pour the batter into the baking pan. Bake for 20 to 25 minutes, until a toothpick poked into the center comes out clean. Cool.

Yield: 8 to 12 pieces

From "Adventures in Corn Meal Cookery!"
Quaker Corn Meal, undated

Orange Bread

*I*n 1865, an Austro-Hungarian stillmaster came to Cincinnati for his sister's wedding. We assume he was happy for her, but he was disturbed by American bread—low quality, he said, because it was made with poor yeast. Charles Fleischmann began to manufacture compressed yeast, which he and his brother then sold door to door by horse and wagon. In 1876, they brought an Austrian baker to the Philadelphia Centennial Exposition; they set up a model Viennese bakery where fairgoers could see, smell, and taste the wonderful things that could be made with good yeast—and they wrapped the yeast cakes in tin foil so they could be shipped anywhere. The horse and wagon were soon history.

Among the wonderful things that can be made with good yeast is this Orange Bread. The pamphlet notes that it's delicious with orange marmalade for afternoon tea. It is also delicious with cream cheese or butter, plain or toasted. It's a lovely golden color, and has a sweet orangey-yeasty smell that is very nice indeed.

1 envelope yeast
¼ cup lukewarm water
2 tablespoons sugar
1 egg, beaten
2 tablespoons melted
   butter

1 teaspoon salt
grated rind of 2 oranges
¾ cup fresh orange juice
3 to 4 cups flour
butter for the mixing
   bowl and baking pan

1. In a mixing bowl, stir together the yeast, water, and 1 tablespoon of the sugar. Let sit for 10 minutes. It should be bubbly and growing.

2. Add the remaining sugar, the egg, butter, salt, orange rind, and orange juice, mixing after each addition. Add 3 cups of flour, mixing well.

3. Turn the batter out onto a floured surface and knead it, continuing to add flour as needed, until the dough is smooth and elastic.

4. Wash and dry the mixing bowl and butter it lightly. Place the dough in the bowl, turn it over, cover the bowl with a clean cloth, and let it sit in a draft-free place until the dough has risen to double its original bulk, about an hour. Poke the dough with your finger-tips—the impression of your fingers should remain in the dough.

5. Punch the dough down, shape it into a loaf, and place it in a lightly buttered 9x5x3-inch loaf pan. Cover the pan with the cloth and let it sit until it has doubled in bulk.

6. Bake at 350 for 1 hour, until the bread is golden brown and sounds hollow when rapped with your knuckles. Remove from the pan and let cool on a rack.

Yield: one loaf

Adapted from "Sunkist Recipes"
California Fruit Growers Exchange, 1916

Sunkist Recipes
Oranges-Lemons

Meat is readily digested because it comes in almost complete contact with the digestive juices. It is 97% digestible. . . .

There was a time when some Americans held the opinion that veal was less digestible than beef or lamb. But research has shown that

Main Dishes

veal acts very much the same in the stomach as do beef and lamb. Occasionally, some individual cannot take care of veal properly, but this may also be true of other foods, and in no way affects the digestibility of veal for persons in general.

"Meat Selection and Preparation," Armour Meat, 1934

Baked Round of Beef with Horseradish

This recipe originally called for a whole bottle of ketchup. (And rings of green pepper with a dollop of horseradish in the center of each, topped with a slice of lemon.) I think ketchup could be one of the great secret ingredients no one tells you about. But a whole bottle? No.

Horseradish, by the by, is in the mustard family, but here it's the root we celebrate and not the seeds. It is undoubtedly called horseradish because it's strong as a wild horse. Cooking tames it. After it's mixed with everything else and has spent its proscribed time in the oven, the horseradish flavor becomes a bit elusive. What we have is more on the pony-radish end of the scale. But still delicious.

1 to 2 tablespoons vegetable oil
2 pounds of chuck, cut into 1-inch cubes
1 medium onion, chopped
1 green or red bell pepper, diced
1 clove garlic, minced
1 tablespoon flour
1½ cups canned tomatoes, chunked

¾ cup ketchup
½ cup water
1 tablespoon grated white horseradish
1 lemon, thinly sliced and quartered
    (discard the end slices, which will be
    all white pith)
salt and freshly ground black pepper

TWO WAYS TO STRETCH BUTTER IN TIMES OF WAR

For our men in service—our Allies—ourselves. Make one pound do where you had two before: Soften 2 teaspoons gelatin in ¼ cup milk; dissolve over hot water. Add 1 ¾ cups top milk (or light cream), gradually beating this into one pound of butter (softened to room temperature but not melted) with rotary beater. When completely blended, beat in 2 teaspoons salt; add 10 drops yellow coloring, if desired. Pack into straight–sided rectangular container; chill until firm. Will keep about a week. Half the amount may be made.

"World War II Recipes," Gold Medal Flour, c. 1942

1. Heat 1 tablespoon of oil in a large oven-proof pan or casserole. Add some of the meat. Don't crowd the pan; remove the meat when browned on all sides, and immediately add more. (Crowding steams the meat instead of searing it.) Add more oil if the pan dries out or the meat sticks. Remove the last pieces of meat from the pan when all have been browned.

2. Add the onion and bell pepper to the same pan, adding more oil if necessary. Cook until the onion is soft and translucent; add the garlic and cook a few minutes longer.

3. Add the flour and cook for 3 minutes, stirring up the browned bits.

4. Return the meat to the pan. Add the tomatoes with their juice, ketchup, and water, and stir well. Stir in the horseradish and the quartered lemon slices. Cover.

5. Bake for 2 hours at 325 degrees, until the meat is fork-tender and the sauce thick. If you need to thicken the sauce further, uncover the pot and cook over medium heat for several minutes. Season to taste.

Serves 6

Adapted from "The Heinz Book of Meat Cookery"
H. J. Heinz Company, 1930

Hungarian Gulasch
(As Prepared by the Hungarian Shepherds)

Before we get to the Hungarian Shepherds, let me note that this recipe is from a very old book that a dear friend has lent me. *The Monarch Cook Book* was published by the Malleable Iron Range Company, makers of Monarch Malleable Ranges, of Beaver Dam, Wisconsin. The book opens with 32 pages about the construction of Malleable Ranges.

Among their advantages, Monarch Ranges had "one thing that every woman appreciates—A TOP THAT REQUIRES NO BLACKING." The upper case letters serve to remind us that women once not only had to keep the fire going, with coal or wood, remove the ashes, and guess at the oven temperature, but also had to polish the stove.

The book includes notes on the design of a model kitchen for an average home. "At the left of the chimney should be a closet for the broom, dust pan, shovel, carpet sweeper, scrub pail, etc....Just inside the pantry door are compartments for flour barrels, above which is a broad shelf and over this may be a cupboard with doors, for cereals such as breakfast foods, tapioca, rice, corn meal, rye, graham, etc....If two maids are kept, there should be a second sink in the china closet or butler's pantry where the dining room girl may wash the better china and silver....The refrigerator should be built in, having thick walls insulated against temperature changes, while the compartment for ice is filled through a small door which opens upon the porch."

As to the Gulasch, as prepared by

the Hungarian Shepherds: "Two hours are required for making this famous Hungarian dish....(It) may be reheated the second day and found quite as good as the first." According to the Malleable Iron Range Company, the Shepherds only used ¼ teaspoon of paprika in their goulash ("More or less paprika may be added as desired"), and they chopped only one small onion. No way! Ask any Hungarian! Or even any shepherd. The best goulashes have equal weights of onions and meat, and a quarter of a teaspoon of paprika is just the beginning for a Hungarian Shepherd.

1½ pounds onions, chopped

2 tablespoons butter

1 tablespoon sweet paprika

1½ pounds beef chuck steak, cut into 1-inch cubes

1 cup canned tomatoes, chunked

1 teaspoon vinegar

5 potatoes, peeled and cubed

boiling water as needed

salt and freshly ground black pepper to taste

1. In a large saucepan or stewpot, sauté the onions in the butter until they are soft and translucent. Add the paprika and continue to cook, stirring, for about 3 minutes so that the paprika will lose its raw taste.
2. Add the beef, the tomatoes, and vinegar. Then, stir, cover, and simmer over low heat for 45 minutes.
3. Add the potatoes and boiling water to cover and cook, uncovered, for half an hour or until the potatoes are soft. The goulash will be liquidy—that's its nature; if you like, you can mash some of the potatoes to thicken it. Season with salt and pepper.

Serves 6

Adapted from "The Monarch Cook Book"
Malleable Iron Range Co., c. 1880

Mrs. Frank Sinatra's Spaghetti and Meat Balls

"The Cook Book of the Stars," a pamphlet published by WFBL radio in Syracuse, New York in 1945, included recipes from a variety of radio personalities. There was a cake recipe from Dick Jones, the actor who played Henry Aldrich on the long-running radio show; newsman Warren Sweeney's cookies (the ingredients included "2 Curtiss 5¢ Baby Ruth bars"); a Date-Fruit Salad Bowl from Johnnie, the Philip Morris cigarette page boy; and Spaghetti and Meat Balls from Mrs. Frank Sinatra. Frank Sinatra was "The Voice" then; in 1945, no one would have known who "Old Blue Eyes" was.

The brief biographical notes with the recipe say, "His mother came to this country from Genoa and his father from Sicily. As a lad, Frank had always been crazy about music, but his parents failed to share his enthusiasm for making a career of it.... The turning point in Frank Sinatra's career came in January, 1943, when he signed for a series of personal appearances at New York's Paramount Theater. Then and there, he became 'The Voice.' Sinatra's slight build is kept in hard trim by his prowess at boxing, golf, and bowling."

MEAT BALLS:	
½ pound ground beef	2 eggs
½ pound ground pork	1 cup bread crumbs
1 clove garlic, finely chopped	1 teaspoon finely chopped parsley
½ cup grated Parmesan cheese	salt and freshly ground black pepper
	olive oil for cooking

1. Mix all ingredients except olive oil. Form into balls (the size of the meat balls is your choice; I prefer something a little larger than a golf ball).
2. Brown the meat balls in olive oil. Remove the meat balls, leaving the oil in the pan, and reserve them to add to the sauce.

TOMATO SAUCE:	
1 small onion, chopped	salt and freshly ground pepper
1 clove garlic, finely chopped	1 teaspoon sugar
1 teaspoon minced parsley	1 large can (1 lb. 12 oz.) Italian-style
1 teaspoon thyme	tomatoes, crushed
	1 large can (15 oz.) tomato puree

1. In the oil remaining from cooking the meatballs, sauté the onion and garlic until the onion is soft and translucent. Add the parsley, thyme, salt and pepper, and sugar, and stir.
2. Add the tomatoes and tomato puree, and stir. Gently add the meat balls to the sauce. Cook over low heat for one hour, stirring occasionally.

| SPAGHETTI: | water |
| 1 pound spaghetti | salt |

1. Cook the spaghetti, according to package directions. Drain.

To Serve

On a large serving platter, place a generous layer of sauce. Add the well-drained spaghetti. Over that goes a generous sprinkling of Parmesan cheese. Cover with more sauce, meat balls, another layer of cheese and a final layer of sauce. Serve immediately.

Note: Mrs. Sinatra strained her tomatoes before she cooked with them. I don't. I like their texture in a smooth sauce. She also removed the onion and garlic from the oil after sautéing them. I can't bring myself to leave out the onions and garlic—I want their flavor, and discarding them also removes too many of the browned bits left from the meat balls. Obviously, Mrs. Sinatra likes a very smooth sauce. Now you know what she did with her sauce that I didn't, and here's what I do that she didn't: I add a teaspoon of sugar. It offsets the acidity of the tomatoes. (As well as the seeds.)

Serves 6 to 8

Adapted from "The Cook Book of the Stars"
WFBL, Columbia Broadcasting System Network, 1945

Baked Pork Chops with Apples

Until relatively recently, when Americans ate meat, they usually ate pork. Pork could be preserved; chicken, beef, and fish could not. Pork can be salted or smoked, and when it's not a fresh roast or chop, it can be used as bacon, ham, and sausage, or to flavor other dishes (like greens and other vegetables), and even to make pie crusts. Almost every part of the pig can be eaten, from the ears to the feet, and on the way, tail and intestines.

In rural areas, people once kept a cow for milk and butter but pigs for meat. Families had pork barrels (for storing preserved pork) in their cellars—thus, "pork barrel legislation," laws passed by congress for the benefit of specific constituents. Other pig-related expressions: "living high on the hog," eating the best of the pork, and "bringing home the bacon," earning what you need to feed your family.

½ cup dry bread crumbs
½ teaspoon ground sage
½ teaspoon thyme
salt and freshly ground black pepper
6 pork chops, center cut, about ¾ -inch to 1-inch thick
3 Granny Smith apples, peeled, cored, and sliced
1 tablespoon butter

1. Preheat oven to 350 degrees.
2. Mix the bread crumbs with the sage, thyme, and salt and pepper. Place in a shallow bowl. Dredge the pork chops, one by one, in this mixture, turning each until it is completely covered. Place the chops in a baking dish.

3. Cover the chops with apple slices and dot with butter.
4. Bake until tender, about 40 minutes.

Serves 6

From "Tappan Cook Book"
The Tappan Stove Company, undated

Luncheon Pork Chops

Luncheon Pork Chops speak of a time when mother cooked a hot mid-day meal every day, father came home from work, the children walked home from school, and the family sat down together to eat—as they did for the morning and evening meals. Were they happier than we are today? Were families less dysfunctional before we had a word for the condition? We'll never know if the good old days were really better, but the pork chops eaten then at lunch can make us happy and functional at dinner.

Pork chops are ready when an instant-reading thermometer registers 160 degrees; or, when you cut into one chop, it shows no pink or just the barest tinge. There are those who say pink pork is not a danger any longer, but it still makes me nervous and I like to feel absolutely safe about my dinner.

1½ cups bread crumbs	2 tablespoons butter, melted
½ cup canned corn	1 egg, beaten
2 tablespoons chopped red bell pepper	¼ teaspoon salt
	freshly ground black pepper to taste
2 tablespoons chopped onion	6 center-cut pork chops

1. Preheat oven to 350 degrees.
2. Mix the bread crumbs with the corn, red pepper, onion, butter, egg, salt and pepper.
3. Place the pork chops in a baking pan. Divide the bread-crumb mixture evenly among the chops, covering each. A bit of water—1 or 2 tablespoons—may be added to the pan to prevent burning.
4. Bake for 40 minutes. If the topping becomes too brown, cover the chops with tin foil.

Note: This amount of topping can be used for four pork chops, or even for two or three—it makes a very generous mound in those cases, and there's nothing wrong with that.

Serves 6

Adapted from "Housewife's Meat Calendar"
National Live Stock and Meat Board, 1929

New York Ham and Beans

"**F**amous Dishes From Every State" was published by Frigidaire in 1936, and it includes a silhouetted map of each of the (then) 48 states, the location of each capitol, the state flower, and a recipe which "to the best of our knowledge" is especially popular in that state. Thus, from South Dakota comes Pheasant Mushroom Delight; from Alabama, Sweet Potato Pudding; and from New York, Baked Ham and Beans. The pamphlet notes that New York Baked Beans are different from "the Boston method which as you know uses molasses." These New York beans use honey. Another difference is that New York Baked Beans include tomatoes and ham; Boston baked beans emphatically do not. Odd that the use of tomatoes is also the main difference between Manhattan Clam Chowder and New England Clam Chowder: One with tomatoes, and the other with cream and salt pork instead. Do New Englanders subconsciously recall the days when tomatoes were considered poisonous? Certainly the timetable for cooking baked beans is a reminder that in Puritan Boston, no one was allowed to cook on the Sabbath. Beans could be baked all day on Saturday; they'd still be warm for breakfast on Sunday and perfectly good for lunch. Housewives sometimes took their uncooked beans to a community oven for all-day baking—reminiscent of Jewish Cholent, pots of beef and beans and vegetables that also need all-day baking (and that were once often taken to community ovens to cook) and is served on the Sabbath, Saturday.

1 pound dried navy beans
1 thick center slice ham
1 medium onion, peeled
½ cup honey
1 teaspoon dry mustard

6 cups water plus ½ cup hot water
   and additional boiling water
1 cup crushed tomatoes
1 teaspoon salt
½ teaspoon freshly ground black
   pepper

1. Rinse the beans, watching for small pebbles. Either soak the beans overnight in water that covers them by 3 inches, or bring the beans and water to the boil, simmer for 2 minutes, remove from the heat, and let stand for one hour. Drain.

2. Add 6 cups water to the beans; bring to a boil, reduce the heat, and simmer for one hour, or until the beans are no longer hard and their skins wrinkle when you dip up a spoonful and blow on them. Drain.

3. Preheat the oven to 325 degrees.

4. Remove as much fat as you can from the ham slice and place the fat in the bottom of a bean pot or Dutch oven. (The pamphlet's recipe calls for a quarter-cup of ham fat.) Add a layer of beans, and place the onion on top of that layer. Cover with the remaining beans. Cut the ham slice in large pieces and bury the pieces in the beans.

5. Mix the honey and mustard with the hot water and pour over the beans. Finally, pour the tomatoes over all. Mix gently. Bake for 4 to 5 hours, checking at intervals to see if the beans are drying out, in which case, add boiling water. The time needed for baking varies. The beans should be soft and tender; cooking them for an additional hour won't hurt them; under-cooking is much worse.

6. Stir in the salt and pepper. Taste carefully, and adjust the seasoning; you may also need more honey or a teaspoonful of sugar.

Serves 6 to 8

Adapted from "Famous Dishes From
Every State"
Frigidaire Corporation, 1936

Ham is one of the best heat and energy producing foods.—Says Royal S. Copeland, Former Commissioner of Health of New York City, now U.S. Senator from New York.

⌐᷈᷉

"60 Ways to Serve Ham,"
Armour, undated

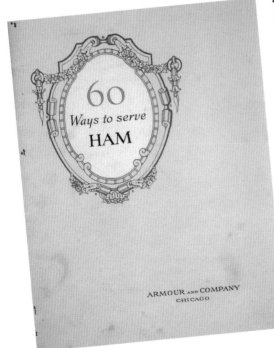

60
Ways to serve
HAM

ARMOUR AND COMPANY
CHICAGO

Chicken Patties

When this recipe was published in 1933, it was called Bunny Sausage, because it was made with rabbit meat. Seems a bit much, if you ask me, to be on nickname terms with your meal. Probably because of our national fondness for Bugs Bunny, Peter Cottontail, and the Easter Bunny, Americans tend to keep rabbit off the dinner table. Chicken is another story. Anthropomorphized chickens are not as cute as bunnies. Chicken Little was disaster-prone, and how many other famous chickens can you think of?

Whatever you call them, these patties are good.

1 pound boneless chicken, ground (ask the butcher to do this for you, or pulse briefly in a food processor)
1 small onion, minced
½ teaspoon salt
½ teaspoon freshly ground black pepper
⅛ teaspoon paprika

½ teaspoon ground sage
½ teaspoon thyme
2 tablespoons chopped parsley
¼ cup bread crumbs, cracker crumbs, or matzo meal
1 egg, lightly beaten
butter for frying

1. Combine all ingredients except the butter. Form into 8 patties.
2. Sauté in butter until browned on both sides.

Serves 4

Adapted from "Kerr Home Canning Book"
Chicago World's Fair Edition, 1933

Roast Sage Chicken with Spinach Dressing

*I*t is difficult to admit this, but there's no sage in the recipe for Sage Chicken as it is published in "Famous Dishes From Every State," a pamphlet issued by the Frigidaire Corporation in 1936. Sage Chicken represents Nevada, so one assumes it's named after the sagebrush that grows wild in the Southwest. On the other hand, it could mean that this is a very wise chicken. And a very surprising one, too, stuffed as it is with spinach. Even so, I think it would be reasonable to add a bit of sage—fresh or dried—to the dressing or to the basting sauce in honor of the state of Nevada.

2 tablespoons chopped onion

6 tablespoons butter

1½ cups chopped, cooked, drained
   spinach

½ teaspoon salt

¼ teaspoon freshly ground black pepper

2 cups bread crumbs

1 roasting chicken

BASTING SAUCE:

½ cup hot water

½ cup melted butter

1 tablespoon Worcestershire sauce

salt and freshly ground black pepper

1. Sauté the onion in 3 tablespoons of the butter until the onion is soft and translucent.

2. Add spinach, salt, and pepper. Cook until the spinach liquid has evaporated. Push the spinach to the side of the pan and add 3 tablespoons butter. When melted, stir in bread crumbs. When the crumbs have absorbed the butter, mix with the spinach. Taste to adjust seasoning.

3. Preheat the oven to 325 degrees. Use the hot spinach mixture to stuff the chicken; sew up or skewer the opening.

4. Roast the chicken for about an hour, until juices run golden and clear when the chicken is pierced with the tip of a knife between the thigh and the body. Baste occasionally with the sauce made of the water, butter, Worcestershire sauce, and salt and pepper.

Serves 4 to 6

Adapted from "Famous Dishes From Every State"
Frigidaire Corporation, 1936

Baked Spring Chicken

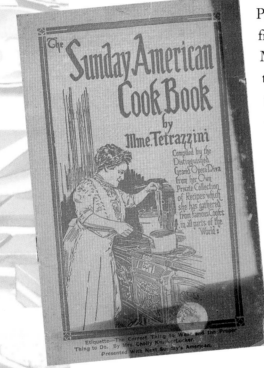

"The Sunday American Cook Book" was the first of a series of pamphlets (later subjects included etiquette, home medicine, jokes, and "physical culture") distributed with a Boston newspaper over several Sundays in 1911. Its recipes, by Mme. Luisa Tetrazzini, were "compiled by the Distinguished Grand Opera Diva from her Own Private Collection of Recipes which she has gathered from famous Cooks in all parts of the World." Wrote Mme. Tetrazzini about her collection, "The artistes of the grand opera, like the birds, fly about to all parts of the earth with the changing of the seasons. We are cosmopolitans, 'citizens of the world,' living from time to time in all the great capitals of modern nations. It is quite natural that we should learn to absorb the excellences of life and customs the world over. And so it is that I have come to have my own standards of what is best in the matter of cuisine..."

The floured and seasoned chicken in her recipe is baked in the oven rather than fried, and it emerges crisp and juicy—more tempting than fried chicken, the recipe says, and I add, without the splatter and fat. Of course, what's substituted for all that fat is cream. As it cooks, the cream reduces, and after you've poured off the yellow fat, you're left with rich curds of flavorful cream. Ah! Once upon a time, cream was supposed to be good for you. Try using evaporated skim milk instead of cream; just bake the chicken without any cream or milk; or you can also remove the skin—the flour seals in the juices. But if you want to taste this chicken as it was once (on a beautiful April day or in the spring of its youth), try it with a cup of cream.

THE AVERAGE OF HUMAN LIFE

The average of human life is about 33 years. One quarter die before the age of six years, one-half before reaching 17. To every 1,000 persons only one reaches 100 years of life. To every 100 only six reach the age of sixty-five and not more than one in 500 lives to 80 years of age. The married are longer lived than the single. Tall men live longer than short ones. Women have more chances of life in their favor before 50 years of age than men have, but fewer afterward. Those born in the spring are generally more robust than the others. The longest lives are found in temperate climates among country people.

**"Guide to Health," Household Instructor
and Family Prize Cook Book, 1898**

1 tablespoon butter for the baking pan
½ cup flour
1 teaspoon thyme
salt and freshly ground black pepper to
    taste

1 chicken, cut into pieces, quarters or
    eighths, as you prefer
1 cup heavy cream

1. Preheat the oven to 350 degrees and butter a baking pan.
2. Put the flour and seasonings in a plastic bag. Shake a few pieces of chicken at a time in the bag—if you're using quarters, do one at a time—and mix well, until the chicken is well coated with the flour mixture.
3. Place the chicken pieces in the prepared pan and bake for 15 minutes.
4. Pour the cream into the pan. Continue baking for 30 minutes, or until the chicken is done.
5. Remove the chicken to a serving platter. Pour off the fat, and scrape up the curds and bits of skin. Add them to the platter, or serve them over rice or mashed potatoes.

Serves 4

Adapted from "The Sunday American Cook Book"
The Boston Sunday American, 1911

Turkey and Peas en Casserole

The subject is leftover turkey. The world's best recipe for leftover turkey, outside of a sandwich, is also the simplest: Mix 3 cups diced turkey with crumbled stuffing (as much as you have, but optimally an equal amount). Mix 2 eggs with 1 cup milk and pour over the turkey in a baking dish. Beat 3 tablespoons soft butter into 2 cups mashed sweet potatoes and add salt, pepper, and nutmeg. Spread this over the turkey, dot with butter, and bake at 375 degrees for 35 to 45 minutes. Serves 6. That's James Beard via Helen McCully. That's for the first night after Thanksgiving. This dish, for the second night, is from a Heinz pamphlet.

There really were 57 varieties of Heinz products once—that was an advertising slogan—and the pamphlet includes a list. First on the list: baked beans. Last: rice flakes. In between: fig pudding, evaporated horseradish, and cooked sauerkraut with pork. And cream of tomato soup, tomato ketchup, and chili sauce. Some things last forever, and some things don't. Leftover turkey doesn't, though sometimes it may not seem that way.

2 tablespoons butter, plus additional butter for the baking dish and for dotting the top of the turkey
2 tablespoons flour
1 cup turkey broth (chicken broth is an acceptable substitute)

¼ cup ketchup
salt and freshly ground black pepper
2 cups cooked turkey (see Note)
1 cup cooked peas
bread crumbs (see Note)
optional: grated Parmesan cheese

1. Preheat the oven to 325 degrees, and lightly butter a baking dish.
2. Melt the butter in a small saucepan; add the flour and cook for 2 or 3 minutes, stirring. Whisk in the broth; then, add the ketchup and salt and pepper, and cook until thickened, whisking often.
3. Place the turkey and peas in alternate layers in the prepared dish and pour the hot sauce over all. Sprinkle with bread crumbs and, if you are using it, the cheese, and dot with the butter.
4. Bake until browned.

Note: Exact quantities don't matter in this dish, and are given only as a guide. The amount of bread crumbs you use depends on the size of your baking dish. You need enough to make a thin crust that covers the top of the turkey and sauce.

Serves 6

Adapted from "The Heinz Book of Meat Cookery"
H. J. Heinz Company, 1930

Baked Fish with Mustard Sauce

Henry J. Heinz began selling pickles to groceries around Sharpsburg, Pennsylvania in 1869—very early in the food revolution that accompanied the industrial revolution. Mr. Heinz and his "57 Varieties" were synonymous with pickles and ketchup for years.

This recipe called for Heinz prepared mustard, number 48 on the list of 57 varieties, which listed brown and yellow mustard as one item, in truth bringing the number to 58. The fish is particularly good with whole grain dijonnaise mustard, and that's what I recommend. And that brings the varieties up to 59.

1½ pounds fillet of salmon, haddock, flounder, or sole, cut into six portions
salt and freshly ground black pepper
1 tablespoon butter, plus butter for the baking pan and for the bread-crumb topping

1 tablespoon flour
1 cup boiling water
1 tablespoon lemon juice
1 tablespoon whole-grain dijonnaise mustard
1 slice bread

1. Preheat the oven to 400 degrees, and lightly butter a baking pan.
2. Dust the fish with salt and pepper and arrange it in the prepared pan.

HOSPITALITY IN WAR-TIME

A Hobo Party—For an evening of fun
Serve supper as a "hand-out" from table on porch or lawn or from inside kitchen
or amusement room table—covered with checkered tablecloth and lined with
leaves or small evergreen clusters. For centerpiece, set up miniature artificial fire
with stewing kettle over it (use lighted electric light bulb under piece of crumpled
red paper for fire—use twigs for props for tiny kettle). Guests find own camping
spots. Supply them with worn tablecloths and napkins well patched in different
colors, tin plates and cups—also for each a bandanna for a knapsack for carrying
food. After supper all sit around open fire—tell stores and sing old-time songs.

"World War II Recipes,"
Gold Medal Flour, c. 1942

3. Melt 1 tablespoon butter in a saucepan. Whisk in the flour, and cook for 3 minutes, stirring frequently. Add the hot water all at once, whisking vigorously. Add the lemon juice and mustard and cook, stirring, until thickened. Pour the sauce over the fish.
4. Lightly butter the bread and pulse quickly in a food processor to make crumbs. (Without a processor, melt the butter and stir in the bread crumbs.) Sprinkle the crumbs over the fish.
5. Bake for 15 to 20 minutes, until the crumbs are lightly browned.

Serves 6

Adapted from "The Heinz Book of Meat Cookery"
H. J. Heinz Company, 1930

CROQUETTES

Once upon a time, white sauce covered everything. Even breakfast.
It was clean and bland (butter, flour, milk), and it blanketed a bevy of sins,
from overcooked vegetables to yesterday's roast. In this sea of white sauce,
there were stepping stones: they were croquettes. Most often made from
leftovers (in the days before refrigeration), croquettes were ubiquitous. Nearly
every cookbook and pamphlet included at least one recipe for croquettes.
But, like white sauce, croquettes were not all bad. Here's how a World War I
pamphlet instructed thrifty cooks to make them.

One cup of any kind of tender cooked meat, or fish, chopped very fine. If you wish the meat to go farther, add an equal amount of mashed potatoes or rice with beef, mutton, or fish; soft bread crumbs or rice with chicken or veal. One or two slices of egg or milk toast that may be left over will take the place of bread crumbs, or you may use any cold meat or fish stuffing. Then you need something to hold the meat together, such as very thick white sauce for light meats and fish, or a brown gravy for beef and dark meat. The yolks of hard-boiled eggs will make the mixture richer, and a raw beaten egg will help to unite the materials. Season to taste, using salt, pepper, lemon juice, parsley, onion juice, mustard, or sweet herbs, but do not over-do it, for it is nicer when the natural flavor of the meat is not wholly disguised.

The mixture should be made quite moist with the thick sauce, because when cold it will thicken considerably, and after frying become soft again. It should be as soft as possible and allow you to shape it like small balls, cylinders, cones, diamonds, or triangles.

Then cover all over with fine dried bread crumbs, dip into beaten egg, and roll in the crumbs again. Fry in smoking hot deep fat, and drain on paper.

"Left Overs—War Edition,"
Hood's Sarsaparilla, c. 1918

Baltimore Crab Cakes

Very often, at the turn of the last century, if you peeked under your white sauce, what you might find was a croquette—a patty of meat, poultry, vegetables, or fish, mixed with various seasonings, egged and breaded and deep fried. Crab cakes descended from the once-ubiquitous croquette. Only they're better.

There are many people who still flour and egg and bread their crab cakes. I really hate that process—my fingers turn into eggplants, and no quick tip for the process has ever helped me. And besides, as we used to say in elementary school, who needs all that? I'd rather taste the crab than the egg and the flour and the bread crumbs and all the hot fat they've soaked up.

This method is gloppy—well, what's perfect?—but it's good.

1 pound crabmeat
½ teaspoon salt
1 teaspoon freshly ground black pepper
1 teaspoon dry mustard
2 teaspoons Worcestershire sauce
1 egg yolk
2 tablespoons mayonnaise

1 tablespoon chopped parsley
optional: 1 tablespoon finely chopped red bell pepper
optional: 1 tablespoon minced or grated onion
optional: ¼ cup bread crumbs
butter for sautéing

1. Pick over the crabmeat and remove any bits of shell or cartilage. Combine the crabmeat with the seasonings, egg yolk, mayonnaise, and parsley. Refrigerate, if possible, for up to 3 hours.
2. Add the red pepper and onion if you're using them. If the mixture seems unbearably loose, add the bread crumbs. Form into round cakes. Refrigerate, if possible, for up to 2 hours.
3. Melt the butter in a frying pan. Add the crab cakes (use a spatula to move them) and sauté them for 2 to 4 minutes, until their bottoms are golden. Turn, and cook for another 3 to 4 minutes. Serve immediately.

Serves 4

Adapted from "Dining Delights"
Colman's Mustard, undated

Fish Curry

*F*rom the Hindu word turcarri—sauce—comes the English word curry. Curry powder is a combination of spices; the selection and proportions vary from region to region and from household to household. Some curries contain more hot peppers than others; some include coconut cream or milk; others vinegar and mustard oil—on and on the variations go.

This is a simple, savory curry from an age when a curried dish ranked with the most exotic of meals. (A recipe for fish curry in a Birds Eye pamphlet published 30 years after this one uses a half teaspoon of curry powder.) What to have with fish curry? Choose from: cucumber mixed with yogurt, peanuts, shredded coconut, chutney, sliced bananas, or just plain rice. But there is no one to say you can't have them all.

2 tablespoons butter, plus butter for the
   baking dish
1 small onion, diced
2 carrots, diced
1 celery stalk, diced
1 apple, peeled, cored, and chunked

1½ tablespoons curry powder
1½ tablespoons flour
1½ cups chicken, fish, or vegetable broth
salt and freshly ground black pepper
1 pound fish (flounder, sole, cod, halibut)

1. Preheat the oven to 350 degrees. Lightly butter a baking dish.
2. Melt the butter in a frying pan and sauté the onion, carrots, celery, and apple until the onion is soft and translucent.
3. Stir in the curry powder and cook for 2 or 3 minutes. Stir in the flour and cook for another 2 or 3 minutes, stirring. Gradually whisk in the broth and cook until the mixture has thickened. Add salt and pepper; taste and adjust the seasoning.
4. Cut the fish into chunks and place in the baking dish. Pour the sauce over. Cover and bake for 15 minutes or until the fish is cooked through. (It will be firm to the touch, and no longer translucent.)

Serves 4

Adapted from "The Sunday American Cook Book"
The Boston Sunday American, 1911

Shrimp Jambalaya

Louisianans are as intense about jambalaya as Texans are about chili or Bostonians about baked beans. Jambalaya is a Cajun-Creole specialty. It usually includes ham; some say the word jambalaya comes from the Spanish *jamon*, or the French *jambon*, both meaning ham, and the Creole word *bal-ayez*, to mix some things together. It's one of those wonderful dishes that can be made with a variety of ingredients, in almost any quantity. It usually includes ham, often chorizo, a Spanish sausage, and always rice. You can make jambalaya with beef, pork, chicken, shrimp, oysters, or crayfish, or a combination; none of those ingredients is more authentic than another. I've used sweet pork sausage here because chorizo can be hard to find; if you can find it, by all means substitute it—sauté it along with the onions—or use both.

1 small onion, chopped

1 clove garlic, minced

1 tablespoon bacon fat, lard, butter, or vegetable oil

1 green or red bell pepper, cubed

1 teaspoon thyme

1 tablespoon chili powder

1 cup rice

1/2 cups canned tomatoes

2 cups chicken broth

few drops Tabasco sauce

salt and freshly ground black pepper

1/2 pound shrimp, shelled and deveined

6 small breakfast sausages, browned separately

1/2 pound ham, chunked

1 to 2 tablespoons chopped parsley, optional, as a garnish

1. Sauté the onion and garlic in the bacon fat until soft. Add the red pepper, thyme, and chili powder and cook for an additional few minutes. Stir in the rice until all the grains are coated.

2. Add the tomatoes with their juice, chicken broth, Tabasco and salt and pepper to taste. Cook for 30 minutes. Meanwhile, brown the sausages in a separate pan. About 10 minutes before the jambalaya is done, add the shrimp, ham, and sausages. Taste and adjust the seasonings. Sprinkle with parsley and serve.

Serves 4

Adapted from "Rice—200 Delightful Ways to Serve It"
Southern Rice Industry, 1935

Russian Salmon

Salmon was called the fish of the czars in Russia, but it's the sour cream that makes this recipe Russian—and delicious. It forms a sweet crust over the salmon, keeping it moist. The lemons become soft and edible—a good foil for the fish.

In 1941, Birds Eye offered more than sixty varieties of frozen foods in the little boxes with the bird logo. Among their advantages were peak flavor, year-round availability, convenience, and no waste: When you bought a box of peas, all you got was peas—when you bought a pound of fresh peas, you paid for the pods and *then* you had to shell them. "When the peas reach flavor peak," the pamphlet reads, "our men hurry out into the fields and harvest them. And here is where the miracle comes in. The button is pressed. And, instantaneously, a blast of arctic cold is released! This cold is so intense that it catches the just-picked flavor at its peak and HOLDS IT IN FOR YOU…" On another page, about spinach, "Claims made for Birds Eye Spinach have been accepted by the American Medical Association."

We've come full circle: peas-in-the-pod are what we cherish now. We always paid for the pods anyway, not to mention the box, the wrapping, and the advertising. Even so, who would give up the freezer and its neat boxes of frozen foods? Not me. A delicious vegetable to accompany this dish is frozen spinach: Coat a small baking pan with olive oil, place an unwrapped block of spinach, still frozen, in the pan, and sprinkle more olive oil on the top. Then bake it along with the salmon. Serve with the blessings of the AMA.

FOR EACH SERVING:
Butter or oil for the pan
1 salmon steak, cut thick
salt and freshly ground black pepper

4 thin slices of lemon, seeds picked out
up to ¼ cup of sour cream (half-and-half is fine, but other low-fat is not)
optional garnish: chopped parsley

1. Preheat the oven to 350 degrees, and butter or oil a baking dish. Place the salmon steak in the dish and sprinkle with salt and pepper.
2. Place the four thin lemon slices on the fish, and top with the sour cream, spreading it so that most of the surface is covered.
3. Bake for 30 minutes, or until the fish is firm and the sour cream is lightly browned. (If you prefer fish rare, bake until it has reached the firmness you like.) Sprinkle with parsley.

Serves 1

Adapted from "Birds Eye Cook Book"
Birds Eye, 1941

Think of serving farm-fresh raspberries in November and field-fresh corn in March! Think of eating ocean-fresh fish thousands of miles from the ocean! Or oysters in the middle of July! Or reveling in chicken as tender as the farmers eat! These are no idle fancies. With Birds Eye they are delicious realities!

**"Birds Eye Cook Book,"
Birds Eye, 1941**

Preserved Sweet Lemons

Lemons preserved in salt are a staple of Moroccan cooking, adding the same salty, tangy zest to a variety of dishes as do olives and capers. Lemons preserved in sugar are much more palatable—softer in flavor but just as intense, sweeter of course, and suitable for a wide variety of dishes. If more were necessary to recommend them, more is available: they are beautiful as they wait in their jar, and they make wonderful gifts. It's strange how they manage to be both exotic and super-American—from a Kerr home canning pamphlet published in 1933.

Some ways to use the lemons: diced and added to chicken, lamb, pork, or fish or a vinaigrette; minced and added, with a little of the syrup, to berries or other fruit. You'll find the taste very intense at first, almost shocking, and at the same time a little elusive—and then you'll find many uses for your golden treasure.

2 whole lemons—organic if possible
1½ cups water
1½ cups sugar

1. Wash the lemons well. Place them in a saucepan, cover with water, and bring to a boil. Simmer them until they can be easily pierced by a toothpick. Drain and let cool.
2. Bring the sugar and the water to a boil and cook until the sugar has completely dissolved.

3. Halve the lemons and add them to the syrup; reduce the heat and simmer for 30 minutes. Turn them at least once as they cook.
4. Place in a hot, clean jar. Cool and refrigerate.

Adapted from "Kerr Home Canning Book"
Chicago World's Fair Special Edition, 1933

Three Mayonnaise Sauces

Richard Hellman was the owner of a New York City delicatessen when he came up with a recipe for a mayonnaise that could be bottled. He found his formula in 1903, and nine years later, in 1912, he began marketing his product. Eventually, he sold his name—and his recipe—to Best Foods of California, thus establishing a new continental divide: east of the Rockies, his bottled mayonnaise is called Hellman's, and west of the Rockies, it is Best Foods.

In a 1941 pamphlet published by Best Foods as a newspaper supplement, there are three wonderful recipes for mayonnaise sauces. Each is good in fish salads, as a sauce for shrimp or other shellfish, an accompaniment to poached salmon, a dunk for raw vegetables, a dressing for vegetable salads, or even a spread for sandwiches.

SNAPPY MAYONNAISE
1 cup mayonnaise
½ cup ketchup
1 teaspoon Worcestershire Sauce
1 tablespoon grated horseradish (white)
dash of Tabasco
½ teaspoon salt
2 teaspoons lemon juice

1. Mix all ingredients together.
Yield: 1½ cups

CUCUMBER MAYONNAISE
½ cup mayonnaise
½ cup chopped cucumber
½ cup sour cream

1. Mix all ingredients together.
Yield: 1½ cups

HORSERADISH MAYONNAISE
½ cup mayonnaise
¼ cup grated white horseradish
2 teaspoons chopped parsley

1. Mix all ingredients together.
Yield: ¾ cup

Adapted from "Hellman's Menu Planner"
Best Foods, Inc., 1941

Escalloped Macaroni with Cheese

Macaroni and Cheese is probably a universal comfort food. It's soft and creamy, it's a beautiful buttery color, and it fills your stomach in a very satisfying way.

There are macaroni and cheese theories. Some recipes call for eggs and cream; others are made just with evaporated milk. The white sauce approach is the most universal, and there is much in its favor. This recipe is in that camp. But however it's made, the most important thing about macaroni and cheese is the cheese. Use good, sharp cheddar. Don't—do not—use anything called "cheese food," which is not cheese and barely food.

Processed macaroni and cheese has been around for a long time. Kraft's famous Macaroni and Cheese Dinner was introduced in 1937, when grandma was a baby. On radio's Kraft Music Hall, it was advertised as a meal for four people that could be ready in nine minutes and would cost nineteen cents. A lot of stores sold it for one thin dime. Two-and-a-half cents per person was a hard price to beat.

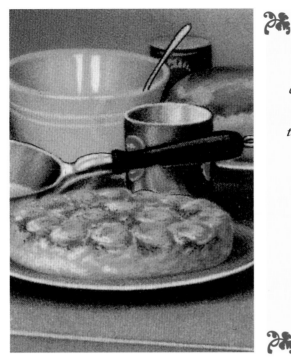

1½ tablespoons butter, plus 1 tablespoon for the baking dish and the topping

1½ tablespoons flour

1½ cups undiluted evaporated milk (skim or regular)

1 teaspoon dry mustard

½ teaspoon sweet paprika

3 cups cooked and drained elbow macaroni

½ pound sharp cheddar cheese, grated

2 slices white bread

1. Preheat the oven to 350 degrees, and use a teaspoon of the butter to grease a medium-sized casserole.

2. Melt 1½ tablespoons of the butter in a medium saucepan. Whisk in the flour and cook for 3 minutes. Add the milk gradually, whisking continuously. Cook until thickened, whisking often. Stir in the mustard and paprika. Add 1¼ cups of the cheese, and stir until it melts.

3. Combine the sauce and macaroni. Place in the casserole, sprinkling the remaining cheese in at intervals.

4. Butter the bread and pulse it quickly in a food processor to make crumbs. (Without a processor, melt the butter and stir in 1 cup of bread crumbs.) Spread the buttered crumbs over the top of the macaroni. Bake until browned, about 35 minutes.

Serves 6

Adapted from "Book of Recipes"
Borden's, undated

Hot Creamed Mushroom Sandwich, Tavern Style

Using hollowed-out bread as patty shells may seem old-fashioned to us now—patty shells themselves are old-fashioned—but this lovely "sandwich" was once very modern. In 1928, the Wonder Bread pamphlet noted that we were entering the third phase of the sandwich—first, there was the bread and beef the Earl of Sandwich ate when he couldn't bear to leave the gaming table for the dining table; second came finger sandwiches, crusts trimmed, filled with "the safe and certain ham or chicken or cheese or jelly....But today," we read, "sandwiches have come into their own.... No occasion is too fine, few meals are too important, for the inclusion of the sandwich." There's the Topless Sandwich, "once known only to the lover of Russian food," the Canapé, and advice about choosing good bread.

Made with Bread

The bread you use matters enormously in this recipe. Try a brioche loaf, Challah, or good bakery white bread. You might also experiment with a loaf of sour dough, or seven-grain bread. You can also vary the mushrooms—use your favorites.

1 loaf unsliced bread	2 tablespoons flour
4 tablespoons butter, melted (you may need additional butter)	2 cups milk
	salt and freshly ground black pepper
1 pound mushrooms, cleaned and sliced	1/2 teaspoon thyme

1. Preheat the oven to 325 degrees. Cut the loaf into four 2-inch thick slices. Remove the crusts and hollow out the insides, leaving a shell to hold the filling. (You can save the bread you've removed for making bread crumbs.) Brush all the surfaces lightly with melted butter. Bake until the shells are golden brown, watching carefully—once they start to brown, they go quickly.

2. In the remaining butter, sauté the mushrooms until they are very lightly browned and have given up their juice. Sprinkle the flour over the mushrooms and cook, stirring, for

GOOD THINGS TO EAT
MADE WITH BREAD

THE FLEISCHMANN CO.

3 minutes. (If the mixture seems too dry, add additional butter, a teaspoon or so at a time.) Quickly add the milk and cook, stirring often, over low heat, until thickened. Add the seasonings.

3. Fill the bread shells to over-flowing with the hot creamed mushrooms and serve immediately.

Serves 4

Adapted from "The Wonder Sandwich Book"
Wonder Bread, 1928

Spinach and Noodle Casserole

eople have been freezing food as a means of preserving it since before the ice age. But procedures were a little haphazard—and depended on wintry temperatures or a steady supply of ice. In seventeenth century England, Sir Francis Bacon died of pneumonia contracted during his attempts to freeze chickens by stuffing them with snow. Clarence Birdseye, a young scientist from Brooklyn, was the first to develop an orderly and less perilous method for freezing food. On an expedition to Labrador for the United States Fish and Wildlife Service in 1914, he noticed that the fish he caught through a hole in the

ice froze the moment they were exposed to air. When he cooked them weeks later,
they still tasted good. He perfected the quick freezing of all sorts of raw and cooked
food. He raised the necessary financial backing and the first Birds Eye packages went
on sale in 1930. The stores willing to stock his frozen foods were given free freezer
cabinets. By the end of the decade, frozen food was a staple across the country.

butter for baking dish
1 10-ounce package frozen chopped
   spinach
1/4 cup boiling water
1 1/2 cups cooked noodles

1/2 cup grated cheddar cheese
2 eggs, lightly beaten
1 1/2 cups milk
1 tablespoon finely minced onion
salt and freshly ground black pepper

1. Preheat the oven to 350 degrees, and lightly butter a medium-sized baking dish.
2. Add the spinach to the boiling water in a saucepan, cover, and cook 5 minutes, or until
   just tender. Drain well. Combine the spinach, noodles, and cheese, and transfer to the
   prepared baking dish.
3. Combine the eggs, milk, onion, and salt and pepper. Pour the milk mixture over the
   spinach and noodles.
4. Bake for 40 minutes, or until a knife poked into the casserole comes out clean.

Serves 4 to 6

Adapted from "Birds Eye Cook Book"
Birds Eye, 1941

*T*o keep vegetables fresh, place them in a deep dish in about two inches of cold water. Take a piece of linen, soak it in water and spread over all, letting the corners dip into the water to keep the cloth moist. Place dish in a window where the air can blow over it.

"Food Economy,"
Knox Gelatin, c. 1895

Vegetables

Baked Carrots and Potatoes

Gail Borden's dream was to find a way to make preservable, portable milk. His first success was with sweetened, condensed milk. (He thought condensation preserved the milk; actually, the heating process destroyed the microorganisms which spoil milk.) In Switzerland, John Meyenberg thought that milk could be evaporated and canned as condensed milk was, but without the sugar. He suggested this idea to his employers, but they weren't interested; eventually, he emigrated to America and established his own company, Helvetia, to rival Borden's. He also helped to found Carnation Milk, which supplied its product in 16-ounce cans to Klondike-bound gold seekers in the gold rush of 1899. Now if those gold diggers and miners had had a few carrots and potatoes and an onion, they could have enjoyed a meal like this one, and stayed to dig another day.

butter for the baking dish, plus 2 tablespoons butter	salt and freshly ground black pepper
4 medium baking potatoes, sliced	½ teaspoon sweet paprika
4 medium carrots, sliced	½ cup evaporated milk
1 medium onion, cubed	½ cup water

1. Preheat the oven to 350 degrees, and butter an 8x8-inch baking dish. Place the vegetables in the prepared dish, and dot with the remaining butter.
2. Mix the seasonings with the milk and water, and pour over the vegetables.
3. Bake, stirring occasionally, until the vegetables are very tender and the top is lightly browned. This will take at least an hour and perhaps longer. You want the potatoes to absorb much of the milk and flavorings; if you use a deep dish this will take longer, but the result will be slightly richer.

Serves 6

Adapted from "Carnation Cook Book"
Carnation Evaporated Milk, 1935

Escalloped Corn

This is the kind of recipe that is usually introduced by saying it's a lovely way to use up leftover bread. Well, it is. It's also a good reason to make fresh, soft bread crumbs in the food processor. The result is rich and quite satisfying.

This early cooking pamphlet from Lydia Pinkham (manufacturer of little pills for women) is devoted largely to a variety of advertisements. The ads are for the the pills and syrups aimed at soothing the problems to which ladies were once prone. "Don't let periodic ailments drag you down," advises one ad. What's remarkable is not the little pills—once the subject of much humor—but the desperate need for euphemisms, even in a pamphlet designed specifically for women. Periodic ailments are the raging hormones of the last generation, and the PMS of today. At least now we've got the initials right.

Ms. Pinkham helped in the kitchen, too. Her pamphlet included several recipes, and her Escalloped Corn could solve a lot of problems about what to have for dinner.

butter for the baking dish, plus 2 tablespoons butter	1 cup bread crumbs
2 cups corn—fresh, canned, or frozen	salt and freshly ground black pepper
	1 cup milk, whole or skim

1. Preheat the oven to 350 degrees, and lightly butter a small, deep baking dish.
2. Place alternate layers of corn and bread crumbs in the baking dish. Dot each bread crumb layer with butter and season with salt and pepper.
3. Pour the milk over all. (It won't reach the top.)
4. Bake for 30 minutes, until the top is lightly browned.

Serves 6

Adapted from "Favorite Recipes"
Lydia Pinkham, undated

Roasted Onions

O nions have been called the truffles of the poor. Certainly, if they were as hard to find as truffles, they'd be valued even more highly than they are. They're desert island food—if you try to think of the five or ten foods you'd take with you to that proverbial desert island, onions must rank close to the top, along with olives, potatoes, tomatoes, and lemons—Wait! that's five and I've barely begun! I think I'll stay here!

When this recipe was published in 1910, I suspect it was taken for granted that the onions would be peeled before they were cooked—the pamphlet doesn't say. But there's no need to peel them, none at all. They cook very nicely in their skins. Roasting unpeeled onions intensifies their flavor and underlines their sweetness. The following directions are for only one serving, but you can make as many as you like, exactly the same way. You'll probably need more than one—these onions are good.

FOR EACH SERVING:
One large onion, unpeeled
butter or oil for the baking dish

unsweetened butter
salt and freshly ground black pepper

1. Preheat the oven to 375 degrees. Place the onion in a saucepan, cover with water, bring to a boil, and simmer for 5 minutes. Drain.
2. Place the onion in buttered baking dish and bake "until it can be pierced with a straw"— until soft and tender—40 minutes to an hour, depending on the size of the onion.
3. Cut a small slice off the top of the onion—or cut a large cross into it, as if the onion were a baked potato. Place a pat of butter and salt and pepper to taste inside the opening and serve immediately.

Adapted from "Gold Medal Flour Cookbook"
Gold Medal Flour, 1910

*T*his recipe is an echo of Tomatoes Provençal—beautiful ripe tomatoes, halved, drained slightly, and topped with bread crumbs, olive oil, and garlic. Mme. Luisa Tetrazzini ("the Distinguished Grand Opera Diva") said that she gathered her recipes from around the world, so perhaps these buttery slices are an Americanized version of that French original. This is not to say they are not delicious, for they are, and it may very well be that Baked Tomatoes have travelled the world, like ravioli, wonton, kreplach, and dumplings, wonderful variations on a single theme. The recipe is way ahead of its time—we have only recently taken to roasted vegetables, with their intense flavor and beautiful colors. The difference between baking and roasting tomatoes is largely one of nomenclature, plus bread crumbs and butter, and bless them both.

butter for the baking dish, plus 2 tablespoons butter
2 tablespoons olive oil

2 tomatoes, stems removed
1/2 cup fresh bread crumbs
salt and freshly ground black pepper

1. Preheat the oven to 350 degrees, and lightly butter or oil a baking dish.
2. Slice each tomato into 4 thick slices. Place the slices in the prepared dish. Season lightly with salt and pepper. Dot with half the remaining butter and oil.
3. Cover the tomatoes with bread crumbs and dot with the remaining butter and oil. Bake 20 to 30 minutes, until lightly browned. Serve hot.

Serves 4

Adapted from "The Sunday American Cook Book"
The Boston Sunday American, 1911

Black Beans Havana—Frijoles Negros

The 1939 New York World's Fair was a last celebration of innocence. Hiltler's menance had become clear. The world believed in the promise of industry, technology, and hard work. There were restaurants from around the world at the Fair, from Albania to Venezuela. These black beans are from the Fair's Cuban Village. There was nothing revolutionary about Cuba then, nor is there now about these black beans. They are traditional, for good reason, because they're good, and they're good *for* you, too.

1 pound dried black beans
1 bay leaf
4 cups water, plus water for soaking
1 or 2 slices bacon, a small piece of salt pork, or 2 tablespoons olive oil

1 medium onion, cubed
2 cloves garlic, minced
1 red bell pepper, cubed
salt and freshly ground black pepper

1. See page 57 for directions for washing, soaking, and initial cooking of dried beans. (One pound of canned beans, drained and rinsed, may be substituted, in which case begin with Step 2.) Drain the beans, add the bay leaf and 4 cups water, bring to a boil, and simmer for an hour, or until the beans are tender and, when you blow on them, their skins wrinkle. Drain, saving about 2 cups of the cooking liquid.

2. Render the bacon or salt pork or heat olive oil in a frying pan. (If you are using bacon or salt pork, remove the meat from the pan and reserve to sprinkle over the beans before serving.) Fry the onion and red pepper in the fat until the onion is soft and translucent; add the garlic and cook a minute or two longer.

3. Add the beans to the frying pan with ½ cup of their cooking liquid (if you are using canned beans, add water); simmer for 30 minutes. The mixture should not be dry—add more liquid as needed. Season to taste. Crush some of the beans to thicken the mixture. Serve with rice. (Remove the bay leaf before serving.)

Serves 8

Adapted from "Food at the Fair, A Gastronomic Tour of the World"
New York World's Fair, 1939

Onion Shortcake

*I*f you love onions, this is for you. And if you love onions, it may please you to know that the Great Pyramids of Cheops at Giza are supposed to have been built by 4,000 stonemasons and 100,000 stonepushers who did all that work on a diet which consisted mostly of chick peas, garlic, and onions.

Don't be put off by this recipe's name; this is a *savory* shortcake. It isn't sweet, except for the natural sweetness of the onions, and it is certainly not garnished with whipped cream. It's delicious; it's handsome; and it'll help you build your own personal pyramid.

ONION FILLING:

2 tablespoons butter

2 Spanish onions, quartered and sliced

1 tablespoon chopped parsley

1/2 teaspoon salt

1/4 teaspoon sweet paprika

SHORTBREAD:

1 cup flour

1/2 teaspoon salt

2 teaspoons baking powder

1 1/2 tablespoons butter, plus butter for the baking dish

1 egg, beaten

1/3 cup plus 1/2 cup evaporated milk, undiluted

Uses for leftover coffee: Make Coffee Jelly, Coffee Spanish Cream, or Coffee Ice Cream. Use in spice cake instead of sour milk or in boiled icing instead of the boiling water for a delicious mocha flavor. It may be used in custards, souffles, or in fudge; it may be added to gravy before removing from the stove, resulting in a rich, dark coloring. Use instead of blueing for khaki goods and also for keeping color in ecru curtains.

"Food Economy," Knox Gelatin, c. 1895

1. Melt the butter and cook the onions in a covered frying pan until they are soft and tender, but not browned. Add the parsley, salt, and paprika. Cool.

2. Preheat the oven to 400 degrees, and generously butter a deep 8-inch pie plate.

3. Make the shortbread: If using a food processor, combine the flour, salt, and baking powder, and pulse in the butter until no large pieces remain; by hand, cut the butter into the flour mixture, using two knives or a pastry cutter.

4. Either by hand or in a food processor, stir half the beaten egg into $\frac{1}{3}$ cup evaporated milk. Stir this into the flour mixture, mixing lightly. Spread this batter over the bottom of the pie plate. Cover with the onions. Mix the remaining half of the egg with the remaining milk and pour this over all.

5. Bake for 25 minutes.

Serves 6

Adapted from "Carnation Cook Book"
Carnation Evaporated Milk, 1935

Rocky Mountain Potatoes

A little potato lore: potatoes came to the old world from the new—from South America to Spain in the sixteenth century. In France potatoes were called *pommes de terre*—apples of the earth; the Dutch called them *aardappel,* or earth apple; similarly, the Germans said *Erdapfel.* This had nothing to do with flavor; it was simply a comparison. There's another story about the names of potatoes: The Spanish soldiers who first saw them growing in South America thought they were a kind of truffle, and called them by the same name, *tartuffo.* In northern Germany, a potato is still a *Kartoffel*; in Russia, *Kartofel*; in Rumania, *cartof.*

Why are these potatoes called Rocky Mountain? I was afraid you'd ask. I don't know. But I do know that they couldn't be simpler, and they are the closest a baked potato will ever get to mashed without taking its jacket off. They're very good.

FOR EACH SERVING:

1 baking potato
1½ teaspoons evaporated milk
1 teaspoon butter
salt
sweet paprika

1. Pierce the well-scrubbed potato with the tip of a knife or the tines of a fork. Bake at 350 degrees until done, about 1 hour. The potato will feel soft when it's squeezed.
2. Cut a wide cross in the potato, and spread the peel back a little. Insert a fork into the opening and mash the potato slightly. Pour in the milk, and poke the butter well into the potato. Sprinkle with a bit of salt and a dash of paprika.

Adapted from "Evaporated Milk Recipes"
Borden's Milk, undated

Potato Hash

Consider hash without the corned beef, or, if you prefer, without the roast beef. That's this recipe. Sort of. There's an extra flourish here: The potatoes are cooked in milk before they're fried. They fry much faster and need less butter, and have a sweeter taste. Save the milk they're cooked in, and add it to soup or chowder instead of cream—it's rich and adds a lovely dimension.

In the pamphlet recipe, a hard-boiled egg was chopped and added to the cooked potatoes. That could be a quick meal for all those nights when there's no corned beef or roast beef in the larder. But more practically, the potatoes without the egg are a very satisfying dish to have when you're in the old-fashioned meat-and-potatoes kind of mood.

It's rarely necessary to peel potatoes. Scrub them well, and cook them virtuously, knowing that most of the vitamins and minerals—and there are lots of them—are clustered right up there under the skin.

4 potatoes, cubed	2 tablespoons butter
1 small onion, cubed	salt and freshly ground black pepper
milk to cover	

1. Put the potatoes and onion in a saucepan and barely cover with milk. Bring to a boil, reduce the heat, and simmer until soft, about 15 to 20 minutes. Drain well.
2. Melt the butter in a frying pan. Add the potatoes, and cook over medium heat, stirring occasionally with a spatula—scraping the bottom and turning the potatoes—until brown. Season to taste.

Serves 4

Adapted from "Tappan Cook Book"
Tappan Stove Company, undated

Sauteed Sweet Carrots

Carrots are naturally sweet. A bit of added sweetening makes them irresistible; like underlining a word, or putting it in italics, it's an emphasis. Molasses is the sweetener in this recipe. Molasses is a by-product of the sugar refining process: it's the syrup that's left over after the sugar has been separated from the juice of the cane. There are differences in molasses because there are different stages in the extraction process. The first produces a light syrup with a mild flavor. The second is darker and has a fuller, richer flavor—that's what's used here. The final extraction results in blackstrap molasses, which is darkest and least sweet and, bitter, in fact.

Strangely, the dark, mellow flavor of the molasses almost evaporates in this recipe. What's left is the emphasized sweet taste of the carrots themselves.

1 pound carrots, scraped
1 tablespoon butter
1 tablespoon molasses
salt and freshly ground black pepper

1. Cook the carrots in lightly salted water to cover until they are almost tender—start testing after 5 to 7 minutes. Remember, they'll cook longer, so they should be on the crisp side of crisp-tender. Drain.

2. Melt the butter in a medium frying pan and stir in the molasses. Add the carrots. Cook until they are tender and lightly browned, about 10 minutes. Season to taste and serve immediately.

Serves 6

Adapted from "Molasses Recipes"
Grandma's Molasses, undated

Summer Squash with Tomatoes

Zucchini does just as nicely as yellow summer squash for this recipe. It's a kind of classic—simple flavors, easy to prepare, good to look at, lovely to taste, and very susceptible to variations. The original pamphlet recipe called for the tomatoes to be seeded and juiced. But I like the seeds—they add texture—and the juice adds moisture as well as flavor. It also directed the cook to cover the baking dish, but cooked that way, the vegetables steam and swim in their juices. Roasting them without a cover intensifies the flavors and adds appealing color to the squash. The dish needs to be watched, though—browned vegetables are good; burnt are not.

For this recipe, you need to peel the tomatoes. It's easy: Either drop them into boiling water for 10 seconds, and then cool them quickly with cold water—the skins slip off easily—or scoop out the stem with a sharp paring knife and peel from there.

2 tablespoons butter or olive oil	1 pound summer squash, cubed
1 small onion, chopped	½ teaspoon oregano
2 tomatoes, peeled and cubed	salt and freshly ground black pepper

1. Preheat the oven to 350 degrees, and lightly butter or oil an 8-inch square baking dish.
2. In a medium frying pan, sauté the onion in the remaining butter or oil until it is soft and translucent. Add the tomatoes and the squash. Sprinkle with the oregano, salt, and pepper, and transfer to the baking dish.
3. Bake for 20 to 30 minutes, stirring from time to time, until the vegetables are lightly browned.

Serves 6

Adapted from "Experts Book on Better Cooking"
Pyrex, 1924

Homemade cake is a real food. Bread has long been a synonym of food, and as cake is a refined, sweetened, and flavored bread, there is no question as to the place cake takes in the dietary. Generously represented in most cakes are the food elements from which our meals are chosen—the protein in eggs, milk, and flour, the carbohydrates in the flour and the sugar, and fats in the milk and butter, the minerals in the eggs and the milk.

Desserts

Because of its high nutritive value, cake is most desirable at a meal that lacks hearty food in the form of meat or fat or their equivalents; but as sugar satisfies hunger almost instantly, cake should be eaten at the end of a meal.

"Cake Secrets," Swans Down, 1919

Bittersweet Chocolate Jewel Cake

*T*his appealing cake has much to recommend it: It's simple, homey, and very good, and it's full of chocolate chips.

Cacao beans—from which comes chocolate—were used as currency by sixteenth century Mayans: A rabbit was worth ten beans; a live slave, a hundred; the services of a prostitute, eight. Columbus brought cacao beans to Spain in 1502. Two Spanish queens, Anne, who married Louis XIII, and the Spanish Infanta, Maria Theresa, bride of Louis XIV, brought to Versailles a chocolate drink made from cacao beans and sugar. Solid chocolate bars became popular in England in the middle of the nineteenth century; the Swiss made the first milk chocolate in 1876; and in 1894, Milton Hershey started using chocolate to coat the caramels he manufactured. Six years later, he sold the caramel business and made his first Hershey bar.

1 tablespoon unsalted butter for the baking pan, plus ½ cup butter	1 cup sugar
2 cups flour	½ teaspoon pure vanilla extract
½ teaspoon salt	3 egg whites
1½ teaspoons baking powder	⅔ cup milk
	8 ounces semi-sweet chocolate chips

1. Preheat the oven to 350 degrees, and butter a 9-inch baking pan.
2. Mix the flour with the baking powder and salt.
3. Cream the butter until it is light; gradually beat in the sugar. Beat in the vanilla. Add the egg whites one at a time, beating after each addition until the batter is light.
4. Add the flour mixture by thirds, alternately with the milk, beating each addition until smooth. Stir in the chocolate chips by hand.
5. Pour the batter into the prepared pan and bake for 50 minutes or until a toothpick poked into the cake comes out clean of batter.

Serves 8

Adapted from "Hershey's Recipes"
Hershey's Chocolate, 1940

As soon as the (cocoa) pods begin to ripen, they are removed with pruning knives, very sharp, and attached to the ends of long poles, which are lengthened by joints as often as required. As the twigs are very tough the blow with this instrument must be strong and well aimed, and the laborers must be experienced on account of the particular skill that is required and the fatigue that attends handling heavy poles sometimes thirty feet long, with the face continually upturned.

"Cocoa and Chocolate,"
Baker Chocolate, 1936

Dutch Apple Cake

*T*he edges of this lovely cake are crisp, almost like a biscuit, but under the apples, it's soft and buttery. The cake is very good plain; would it be better with a bit of whipped cream or a scoop of vanilla ice cream? What wouldn't be? By itself, though, it has a sweet simplicity that is very appealing.

1 tablespoon unsalted butter for the baking pan and ½ cup plus 2 tablespoons unsalted butter

2 cups flour

½ teaspoon salt

4 teaspoons baking powder

1 egg, beaten

¾ cup milk

6 peeled, cored, and sliced firm, tart apples, such as Granny Smith

½ cup sugar

½ teaspoon cinnamon

¼ teaspoon grated nutmeg, fresh if possible

1. Preheat the oven to 350 degrees, and butter an 8-inch square baking pan.
2. In a food processor, mix the flour, salt, and baking powder. Pulse in the ½ cup of butter. Add the egg and milk, and pulse again, until the batter is just mixed. (By hand, cut the butter in with a pastry cutter or two knives, and moisten with the egg and milk.)
3. Scrape the batter into the pan, pushing it so that the bottom of the pan is evenly covered, and some of the batter comes up the sides. (The batter is very sticky.)
4. Cover with the apple slices, arranging them in rows or in circles.
5. Mix the sugar with the spices and sprinkle this mixture over the apples. Dot with the remaining 2 tablespoons butter.
6. Bake for 30 minutes, until the apples and cake are lightly browned.

Serves 8

Adapted from "Fruit Cook Book"
Rumford Baking Powder, 1927

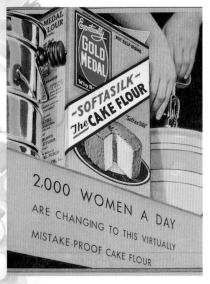

Lemon Cottage Cheese Cake

Cheese cake can be smooth, unctuous, and creamy—when it's made with cream cheese; that's what's called New York Cheese Cake (everywhere except in New York). Lindy's famous cheesecake was the smooth kind, and so is Sara Lee's. It can also be lumpy and bumpy—when it's made with cottage cheese or ricotta, as is Italian cheese cake, or this lovely Cottage Cheese Cake. My mother made the best cheesecake I've ever tasted. It was lumpy and bumpy, and no one has her recipe. This comes close, and so I like it very, very much.

¼ cup unsalted butter, plus additional
    butter for the baking pan
bread crumbs for the baking pan
¾ cup sugar
4 eggs, separated
grated rind of 1 lemon

1 teaspoon lemon juice
2 cups cottage cheese (one pound)
¾ cup cake flour
½ cup heavy cream
pinch of salt
dash of cream of tartar

1. Preheat the oven to 325 degrees. Butter a 2- or 3-inch-deep baking pan, and dust with bread crumbs.
2. Cream the butter. Gradually add the sugar and continue beating until light. Add the egg yolks one at a time, beating after each addition. Add the grated rind and the lemon juice and mix well.
3. In a separate bowl, add the cottage cheese to the flour and stir in the cream. Combine well.
4. Add the cheese mixture to the butter mixture and stir thoroughly.
5. Using a clean bowl and beaters, beat the egg whites until foamy. Add the salt and cream of tartar and continue to beat until the egg whites are stiff but not dry. Fold into the cheese batter.
6. Pour the batter into the prepared pan, and bake for about 1½ hours, or until the cake feels firms to the touch. Cool in the oven with the door ajar.

Serves 8 to 10

Adapted from "The Complete Cottage Cheese Recipe Book"
Pennsupreme, undated

Some of us like swing music, and some like old-fashioned songs. But it's music to any woman's ears to hear: "This is the best cake I ever tasted!"

**"Kate Smith's Favorite Recipes,"
Calumet Baking Powder,
1939**

Pound Cake

A pound each of flour, butter, eggs, and sugar: These are the traditional ingredients for pound cake, plus a pinch of salt and a bit of vanilla. Most pound cake recipes nod to tradition by keeping the name, but then change the ingredients. This one is no different, except that it goes a little further than most. The eggs are separated and the whites beaten and then added, and there's lemon extract as well as vanilla. The result is a light cake with a slightly lemony flavor. It's still buttery and delicious and relatively simple to prepare.

unsalted butter for the pan plus one cup
   at room temperature
1 cup sugar
1 teaspoon pure vanilla extract

1 teaspoon pure lemon extract
5 eggs, separated
2 cups flour
1 teaspoon baking powder

1. Preheat the oven to 325 degrees, and butter a 9x5x3-inch loaf pan.
2. Cream the butter. Gradually add the sugar, beating well until it is incorporated. Add the two extracts and beat in. Add the egg yolks, and continue to beat until the batter is pale yellow.
3. Using a clean bowl and beaters, beat the egg whites until they are almost stiff—light and very foamy, but not dry. Mix the flour and baking powder in a separate bowl. Add the flour mixture to the batter by thirds, alternating with the egg whites (begin with the whites). Beat well for several minutes; the batter should be light.
4. Pour into the prepared pan and bake for about 1 hour, until the top is lightly browned and the cake tests done—a toothpick poked into the middle of the cake should come out clean.

Serves 8 to 12

Adapted from "Royal Cook Book"
Standard Brands Incorporated, 1930

Queen Anne Apple Flamri

I love the name of this recipe. Flamri is probably derived from "flummery," an old word for a custard or fruit pudding or a gruel made from oats that goes back to the 1700s. From flummery to flamri is probably just a small regional stretch. Queen Anne could be the early eighteenth century English queen—or perhaps just a kind of apple.

The pamphlet calls for baking the Flamri in a "tart-paste" but I think it does better by itself—its pudding-like texture doesn't benefit from a pie crust, and why eat a pie crust if it doesn't benefit?

There are about 90 recipes in the pamphlet from which this recipe comes, and only six of them merited editorial comments—like "fine," or "very fine," or, in one instance, "cheap." Queen Anne Apple Flamri is, according to the pamphlet—and to me—"delicious."

Do not attempt shortcake unless you can do it correctly. If you have not plenty of berries, and if you cannot make a rich, light and crisp shortbread crust, serve your berries plain, instead of adding to your list of failures.

"Reliable Receipts,"
Reliable Flour, 1902

1 teaspoon butter for the pan	¼ teaspoon cinnamon
6 apples, peeled, cored, and sliced thin	2 tablespoons flour
3 tablespoons dried currants	¼ teaspoon baking soda
3 tablespoons, plus ¼ cup sugar	1 cup of sour cream
2 eggs, beaten	

1. Preheat the oven to 375 degrees, and butter an 8-inch square shallow baking pan.
2. Mound the apples in the baking pan. Sprinkle with the currants and 3 tablespoons of the sugar. Bake for 10 minutes.
3. Meanwhile, mix the eggs, remaining sugar, cinnamon, flour, baking soda, and sour cream. At the end of the 10-minute baking time, pour this egg mixture over the apples.
4. Continue to bake for 20 minutes, or until lightly browned.

Serves 6

Adapted from "Cook Book and Facts Worth Knowing"
Cow Brand Soda, 1913

Fall Squash Pie

S quash Pie is close kin to Pumpkin Pie. It's made with winter squash—acorn, butternut, hubbard, or, for that matter, sugar pumpkin. What makes this recipe special is that the spices are limited—you use either a *small* amount of cinnamon, *or* nutmeg, *or* ginger, with a resulting pie filling that tastes of squash, rather than the cover-all flavor of spices.

The word squash is interesting. It can refer to vegetables as different as zucchini and butternut, or a game, or an English cold drink, or what happens when you inadvertently sit on the pie. This pie is as unusual as it is good, so please don't sit on it. You would squash the Squash Pie, and waste a delicious dessert.

1½ cups cooked squash (if you use frozen squash, simply defrost)
⅓ cup sugar
¼ teaspoon salt
¼ teaspoon cinnamon *or* freshly grated nutmeg *or* ground ginger

1 egg, beaten
1 cup milk
unbaked 9-inch pie shell

1. Preheat the oven to 375 degrees.
2. Mix the squash, sugar, salt, cinnamon, egg, and milk until well-blended.
3. Pour into the pie shell. Bake for 30 to 40 minutes, until the crust is brown and the filling is lightly browned and no longer jiggles. If the crust browns too quickly, reduce the heat to 350 degrees.

Serves 8

Adapted from "Home Cooking Album"
Wilkin Whiskey, 1935

Chocolate Bittersweet Cookies

HERSHEY'S RECIPES

The chocolate chip cookie story goes like this: In 1795, Amelia Simmons's *American Cookery* became the first cook book to be published in America. One of its recipes was for a lovely cookie made with both brown and white sugar.

Now it's 1933. Ruth Wakefield is baking a batch of cookies for the inn she and her husband own. Her recipe is almost exactly the same as Amelia Simmons's. But she wants to bake *chocolate* cookies, and she's in a rush. She decides that if she adds chopped chocolate pieces to the batter, the chocolate will melt in the oven and she'll have saved the time involved in melting it separately. But the chocolate doesn't melt—it stays in separate pieces—and the cookies are wonderful. She names them after her Toll House Inn. Six years later, Nestlé starts distributing chocolate that is *already* chopped. The company buys the rights to the Toll House name and recipe, and packages its chocolate bits in a cellophane bag with a picture of the Toll House Inn in the corner.

And a year after *that*, Hershey publishes its pamphlet of chocolate recipes, including one for chocolate chip cookies that is almost exactly the same as the Nestlé recipe—which is almost exactly the same as the Amelia Simmons recipe—but changes its name to Chocolate

Chocolate soothes both stomach and brain, and for this reason, as well as for others, it is the best friend of those engaged in literary pursuits—Baron Von Liebig

"Cocoa and Chocolate," Baker Chocolate, 1936

Bittersweet Cookies. A cookie by any other name, Shakespeare almost said, still tastes as sweet.

In 1940, when this recipe was published, Hershey's wasn't making bittersweet bits—the recipe includes directions for breaking an eight-ounce bar of Hershey's bittersweet chocolate into little bitty pieces, and a note that if you'd rather have milk chocolate cookies, you could chop up a large bar of Hershey's milk chocolate to use instead.

1 cup flour	¼ cup granulated (white) sugar
1 teaspoon baking powder	1 egg
⅛ teaspoon salt	½ teaspoon pure vanilla extract
½ cup butter, at room temperature	⅓ cup walnut pieces
½ cup brown sugar, packed	8 ounces semi-sweet chocolate chips

1. Preheat the oven to 350 degrees.
2. Mix the flour, baking powder, and salt in a small bowl.
3. Cream the butter with the two sugars until it is light and fluffy. Beat in the egg and vanilla.
4. Gradually beat the flour mixture into the butter mixture. Add the nuts and the chocolate and combine thoroughly.
5. Drop by rounded tablespoons onto an ungreased cookie sheet.
6. Bake for 10 minutes, or until golden brown. Let stand on the sheet for 2 or 3 minutes before transferring, with a spatula, to wire racks to cool.

Yield: two dozen cookies

Adapted from "Hershey's Recipes"
Hershey Chocolate Corporation, 1940

Corn Meal Cookies

A cookie is not a cookie the whole world 'round. In England, a cookie is a cake or a biscuit, depending. In Scotland, a small bun is what goes so nicely with a glass of milk. Our word "cookie" is not what it seems, either: It comes from the Dutch *koekje*, which means little cake.

Whatever they're called, cookies are wonderful. You can have one for each hand. You don't get icing on your fingers. They go as well with afternoon tea as they do with an apple. Children love them. And some of us never grow up. Cookie-wise, at least. Corn Meal Cookies are for adults as much as for children. They're crisp, not too sweet, and have a wonderful corn meal crunch and an elusive lemony flavor.

1 cup butter	1 teaspoon baking powder
1½ cups sugar	½ teaspoon salt
2 eggs	1 teaspoon freshly grated nutmeg
1 teaspoon pure lemon extract	1 cup corn meal
3 cups flour plus extra flour for rolling out the dough	½ cup raisins

1. Preheat the oven to 400 degrees.
2. Cream the butter and gradually add the sugar, beating well. Beat in the eggs one at a time and continue beating until the batter is light and fluffy. Add the lemon extract.
3. Mix the flour with the baking powder, salt, nutmeg, corn meal, and raisins and add gradually to the creamed mixture. The batter will become very stiff; if you're using a mixer, you may have to finish with your hands.
4. Sprinkle a rolling-out area with flour, and flour your rolling pin. Pat down the batter and turn it over so that both sides are floured. Roll out the dough to a thickness of ⅛-inch. Cut with a floured cookie cutter or a 2-inch biscuit cutter.
5. Place the cookies on an ungreased baking sheet and bake for 10 to 12 minutes, watching carefully. The cookies should be very lightly browned; the edges will be a little darker. Use a spatula to transfer the cookies to a rack to cool.

Yield: 3 dozen 2-inch cookies

Adapted from "Adventures in Corn Meal Cookery"
Quaker and Aunt Jemima Corn Meal, undated

Walnut Sticks

"Sticks" sounds crisp and dry, but *these* sticks are really bars, soft and chewy, and with crunch from the nuts. They have a rich flavor, but there's no butter in the dough—you need just a bit to butter the pan. And you'd have to devour half of the recipe in order to consume one of the two eggs. Not to say that couldn't be done—a Cookie Monster could easily eat them all.

butter for the pan
1 cup loosely packed brown sugar
½ cup flour
¼ teaspoon salt
½ teaspoon pure vanilla extract
2 eggs, well beaten
1 cup chopped walnuts

1. Preheat the oven to 375 degrees, and butter an 8-inch square shallow baking pan.

2. Add the brown sugar, flour, salt, and vanilla to the eggs and stir well. Stir in the walnuts.

3. Pour into the prepared pan and bake for 20 to 25 minutes. While still warm, cut into bars, and remove from the pan.

Yield: 12 bars

Adapted from "To Win New Cooking Fame"
Diamond Walnuts, undated

Chocolate Bread Pudding

*P*udding is such a plebian word—it has a plodding, thudding sort of sound; you might expect puddings to be thick and dumpy and dull. But no! Puddings may not be soufflés, all fluff and foam; puddings may not be *petit fours*, dainty and decorated; puddings may not be meringues, lighter than kisses (and equally unreliable). But puddings will be there, sturdy and strong, when your soufflé has collapsed; puddings will be there, solid and safe, when your *petit fours* have disappeared in a bite and a half; puddings will be there, comforting and reliable, when your meringues have crumbled apart and your love has flown. Puddings are home.

Bread pudding is one of the best. And Chocolate Bread Pudding is what happens when bread pudding gets big ideas. Are you listening, chocoholics?

butter for the baking dish	¾ cup sugar
4 cups bread, in slices or large cubes (see Note)	2 eggs, beaten
4 cups milk (whole or low fat)	¼ teaspoon salt
2 squares unsweetened chocolate	1 teaspoon vanilla extract

1. Preheat the oven to 350 degrees, and butter a baking dish. (The larger the dish, the crisper the bread. An 8-inch square baking dish results in a crisp top and a soft bottom.)

2. Optional: Many people like to soak the bread in the milk for half-an-hour before combining the ingredients. This makes a very soft pudding. If you like your pudding soft, place the bread in a mixing bowl, pour the milk over, and soak for 30 minutes. Otherwise, skip this step.

3. Combine the milk and chocolate in a double boiler or an oven-proof pan. Cook over low heat or in a slow (250 to 300 degree) oven until the chocolate has melted. (If you've pre-soaked the bread, pour off the milk in order to warm it.) Whisk the sugar, eggs, vanilla, and salt into the melted chocolate and milk.

4. Arrange the bread in the baking dish, overlapping the slices. Pour the milk mixture over the bread. Let stand for a minute or two. Bake for 1 hour.

Note: Much depends on the kind of bread you use. A good bakery bread—a day-old French or Italian loaf without seeds—makes a lovely pudding of substance.

Serves 8

Adapted from "Good Things to Eat"
The Fleischmann Company, 1912

Pineapple Bavarian Cream

Just before the turn of the last century, a couple in upstate New York sold the rights to a flavored and sweetened gelatin dessert to the Genesee Pure Food Company. The price for this corporate birth of Jell-O was $450. In 1925, Genesee, now the Jell-O Company, was sold to Postum (which later became General Foods). A year before that sale, in 1924, Genesee published a little pamphlet called "A Jell-O Year." It has a hole in the corner for a string, for hanging from a kitchen nail, and features "The Jell-O Girl," an angel with a Dutch bob.

According to the pamphlet, The Jell-O Girl says that each of her recipes is easy to make—"for she has always insisted that her recipes should not be 'fussy' or bothersome." The Jell-O girl makes daisy chains in May, has a tea party for her dolls in June, and studies geography in September. In August, she goes swimming. And afterwards, she eats Pineapple Bavarian Cream. Lucky girl! Pineapple Bavarian Cream is as good in February as it is in August, and that's very good indeed. The pamphlet called for whipped Jell-O to be accompanied by whipped cream, but the whipped cream is better inside, really it is—and I recommend it all year long.

1 3-ounce package lemon Jell-O
1 cup boiling water
1 15-ounce can of crushed pineapple, in its own juice, strained (reserve both juice and pulp)
1 cup heavy cream, whipped until very thick

1. In a heat-resistant mixing bowl, stir the Jell-O in the boiling water until completely dissolved. Add 1 cup of the juice from the pineapple. (Drain as much juice as possible from the pineapple—you'll have slightly more than a cup but only use one cup.) Chill.

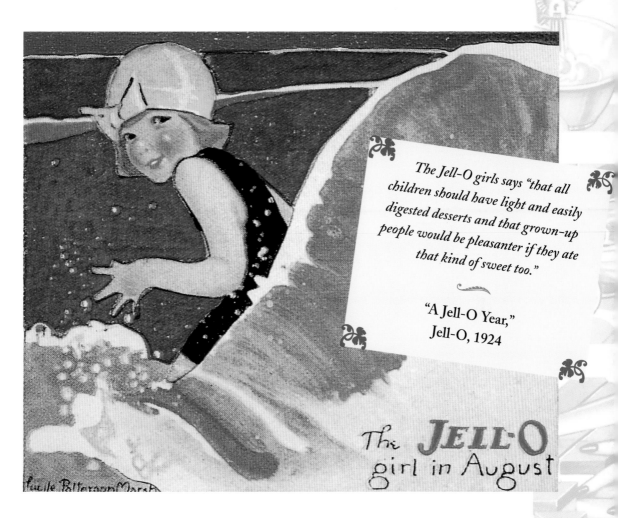

The Jell-O girls says "that all children should have light and easily digested desserts and that grown-up people would be pleasanter if they ate that kind of sweet too."

"A Jell-O Year,"
Jell-O, 1924

The JELL-O
girl in August

2. As soon as the Jell-O is syrupy, about an hour after it has been refrigerated, pour it into a large mixing bowl and whip it until it is thick and frothy. Combine with the whipped cream. Fold in the reserved strained pineapple.

3. The dessert can be poured into a water-rinsed mold. (Later unmold by dipping quickly into hot water.) If you'd rather not fuss with unmolding, pour the mixture directly into a bowl, glass if possible—it's a pretty, pale yellow. Refrigerate 4 hours or until firm. Serve with a few raspberries, strawberries, cherries—even blueberries!—scattered over it.

Serves 6

Adapted from "A Jell-O Year"
Genesee Pure Food Company, Jell-O, 1924

AMERICA'S MOST FAMOUS DESSERT

JELL-O

NET WT   3¼ OZS.

A MIXTURE

DELICATE   **DELIGHTFUL**   **DAINTY**

STRAWBERRY

PURE FRUIT FLAVOR

VEGETABLE COLOR

THE GENESEE PURE FOOD CO. LE ROY, NEW YORK

No matter where
you live you get this
perfect package of
JELL-O
at
all times of the year

Mint Jell-O

At last! A way to use all that out-of-control mint in the garden! The original recipe used lemon Jell-O—lime hadn't been produced yet—but lime is much better for the mint because it *looks* right. The pamphlet includes sample menus, and one suggests serving this with lamb chops. I think it makes a very refreshing dessert.

¼ cup white vinegar
2 tablespoons sugar
1¾ cups water

½ cup fresh mint leaves, packed
1 3-ounce package lime Jell-O

1. Combine the vinegar, sugar, and water and bring to a boil. Stir in the mint leaves and boil for 1 minute longer.
2. Put the Jell-O in a medium, heat-resistant mixing bowl and strain the boiling mint mixture into it. Stir until the Jell-O is dissolved. Pour into a water-rinsed mold. (Later, unmold by dipping the mold quickly into hot water.) If you'd rather not fuss with unmolding, pour the Jell-O directly into a serving bowl. Chill 4 hours or until firm.

Serves 4

Adapted from an untitled pamphlet of Jell-O recipes
The Jell-O Company, Inc., 1925

Old-Time Refrigerator Pudding

*T*his simple, summery, and old-fashioned dessert is a favorite English sweet; its name is really Summer Pudding. Gold Medal must have renamed it in 1942 in order to emphasize the still relatively new refrigerators. Whatever you call it, it's full of the best flavors of summer. The only hitch is that you have to wait a day to eat it, but it's all the better for that.

6 to 7 cups berries (See Note)
¾ to 1 cup sugar (depending on the sweetness of the berries)
about 24 slices firm white bread (such as Pepperidge Farm or Arnold's), crusts removed
whipped cream, crème fraîche, or yogurt

1. Combine the berries and sugar in a large saucepan and cook over medium heat until the berries are juicy, about 5 minutes. Taste for sweetness—add more sugar if you feel it's needed.
2. If you want a molded pudding, line a mold with plastic wrap and let a short length hang over the sides. Line the sides and bottom of the mold or a serving bowl with bread slices cut into triangles and rectangles. Make sure they completely cover the bowl; if not, cut a piece of bread to fit the hole and work it into place.
3. Spoon about half the berries into the mold; cover with a layer of bread; add most of the remaining berries, reserving a small amount, and top with a final layer of bread. Cover with plastic wrap. Put a flat plate, large enough to cover the surface of the pudding, on the top, and set a 2- to 3-pound weight (a large can of tomatoes, for instance) on the plate. If the bread reaches to the top of the mold, use another plate underneath the mold to catch possible drips. Refrigerate overnight.
4. Unmold if desired. If there's any bread that hasn't soaked up berry juice, spoon the reserved berries over it. Serve with whipped cream.

Note: Raspberries and currants are the most traditional fruits, but you can use all raspberries, or almost any combination of berries: blackberries, strawberries, loganberries, even blueberries—or *just* blueberries.

Serves 6 to 8

Adapted from "World War II Recipes"
Gold Medal Flour, 1942

Berry Cream

This recipe was published in 1932, when frozen desserts had status—you had to have a refrigerator (not an ice box) in order to make it. But its heritage is very clear, once it thaws. This is an old Fool (than which there is no fool like). A Fool (the dessert goes back several centuries) is cooked, strained fruit folded into whipped cream. In 1932, Birds Eye, looking for ways to use frozen raspberries, hit upon the marvelous idea of freezing the Fool.

Berry Cream can be made with any berries—raspberries, strawberries, blueberries, blackberries—and probably with peaches or plums or almost any kind of fruit. Blackberries make a particularly lovely dish because their color is so intense.

1 12-ounce package of unsweetened
   frozen berries
¼ cup sugar

1 teaspoon lemon juice
1 cup heavy cream
pinch of salt

1. Put the berries in a medium saucepan with the sugar and 1 or 2 tablespoons of water. Cook over gentle heat until the berries are soft and very juicy.
2. Strain into a bowl, pressing the berries against the sieve with the back of a spoon. Add the lemon juice to the purée. Taste, and if necessary, add more sugar or lemon juice.
3. Whip the cream, adding the pinch of salt. When it holds soft peaks, whip in most of the fruit purée, reserving about ¼ cup to use as a sauce.
4. Place the berry cream in the freezer for a minimum of 4 hours. Stir at least once while the dessert is freezing.
5. Remove from the freezer about 15 minutes before serving. Spoon into dessert dishes, and serve with the reserved sauce.

Note: Berry Cream can be served unfrozen, with the bit of reserved fruit juice over it. It is excellent this way—berry-whipped cream—sheer indulgence. And the stewed strained berries alone make a lovely sauce if you don't press them hard while you sieve. Unfrozen Berry Cream is also a lovely sauce for fresh fruit or cake.

Serves 4

Adapted from "20 Minute Meals"
Birds Eye, 1932

Frozen Sicilian Chocolate Mousse

The next time you have a good idea, think of this: In 1876, 18-year-old Milton Snaveley Hershey borrows $150 from his aunt to open a shop in Philadelphia in order to sell the penny candy he makes. It doesn't do well, so in 1883, he gives up, moves to New York City, works for someone else, and then opens a small caramel factory. Three years later, he's bankrupt. He goes back to Pennsylvania and, with the help of his aunt and his mother, starts over again, this time making tissue-wrapped caramels. He almost goes under again, but in 1891 his cousin invests in the company. Hershey decides to dip his caramels in chocolate. Three years later, he's grossing nearly a million dollars annually. Eventually his name will become synonymous with chocolate. Well, not Snaveley. Just Hershey.

This Chocolate Mousse is lovely on a hot day: It's simple, sweet, cold, and chocolate. What more could you ask for?

2 cups heavy cream
½ cup powdered sugar
2 tablespoons chocolate syrup
¼ cup chopped pecans

1 teaspoon pure vanilla extract
optional garnish: grated chocolate,
chocolate sprinkles, or whole pecans

1. Whip the cream in a medium bowl, and when it has thickened add the sugar and syrup. Continue whipping until thick and firm (watch carefully; if you over-whip it, you'll have butter). Add the pecans and the vanilla, and combine thoroughly.

2. Pour into a mold or serving bowl and freeze. Either unmold or serve from the bowl. If you like, garnish with grated chocolate or chocolate sprinkles or whole pecans.

3. Before serving the mousse, let it stand for about 15 minutes at room temperature in order to soften slightly.

Note: Dark Semi-Sweet Syrup is especially good.

Serves 4 to 6

Adapted from "55 Recipes for Hershey's Syrup"
Hershey Chocolate Corporation, undated

IT WAS WAR THAT "GAVE BIRTH TO THE ART OF CANNING"

So says the "Canned Food Manual," a small book about cans prepared in 1942 by the American Can Company for the United States Army.

The American Can Company tells us that during the winter of 1795, a shortage of fresh fruits and vegetables caused an outbreak of scurvy among the French soldiers. Desperate, Napoleon offered an award of 12,000 francs to anybody who could come up with an improved method of preserving food. Voila! A French brewer and confectioner found a way to preserve food by boiling it in jars, which he then sealed with corks and tar. He won the money, and his process was declared a French military secret. But across the Channel, an enterprising Englishman soon found another way to preserve food—in tin-plated steel containers. Cans came before can openers: Until 1865, what you used to open a can was simply a hammer and a chisel.

The manual mentions that wars advance the art of canning because of the need to feed "large concentrations of men..." who are probably far from usual food sources. It describes the advances in canning each American war has seen, from processing food at higher temperatures (discovered during the Civil War), to condensed milk (the Spanish-American War), and the perfection of the modern can (World War I).

"Canned Food Manual," American Can Company, 1942

Photograph of Douglas Fairbanks, Jr. "Favorite Recipes of the Movie Stars," 1931

ON SERVING GELATINE DISHES

At breakfast it is often desirable to serve the juice of oranges, grapefruit, or lemons, with or without the pulp, or with the addition of a few strawberries, slices of peaches, or bananas, in the

form of a jelly. As the acid of fruits is liable to impede the digestion of starch, the choice of jelly or cereal should be given. If this course is to be served at the table, the jellied fruit and cereal are placed before the mistress, and the waitress or butler, standing at the left, sets before her two "change" plates, one holding a chilled plate for the jelly and the other a warmed saucer for the cereal. The hostess or waitress ascertains from which dish the individual at the right of the hostess desires to be served, and when the mistress has served this article, the waitress lifts the plate with the right hand and replaces it with a second change plate holding a chilled or warmed saucer, as is needed. With the left hand the plate in front of the guest is taken up and replaced by that prepared by the mistress, and the cream and sugar are passed to the left on a tray; in like manner, passing to the right of the hostess, others are served. When this course is finished, remove the plates from the left, one at a time, or one in each hand, leaving the "change" plate before each guest or individual.

"Dainty Desserts for Dainty People,"
Knox Gelatin, 1901

Art Credits

"A Jell-O Year—1924," The Genesee Pure Food Company, LeRoy, NY, 1924: jacket, cover, xviii (bottom), xix (top), 111, 112

"A Selection of Choice Recipes," Rumford Baking Powder, Providence, RI, undated: 94

"Adventures in Corn Meal Cookery," Quaker and Aunt Jemima Corn Meal, undated: 40

"Aladdins Lamp At Mealtimes," Francis Leggett & Company, New York, NY 1927: 23 (bottom)

"Any One Can Bake," Royal Baking Powder Co., 1929: 107

"The Associated Customer," New York State Electric Co., 1929: 92 (bottom)

"Ayer's Preserve Book," Dr. J.C. Ayer & Co., Lowell, MA, undated: jacket spine

"The Ball Blue Book," Ball Brothers Company, Muncie, IN, 1934: dedication, 86

"Bananas in the Modern Manner," Banana Growers Association, New York, NY, 1930: 19, 35

"Be An Artist at the Gas Range," Longmans, Green, & Co., 1935: 2

"Beardsley's Helpful Suggestions," J.W. Beardsley's Sons, Newark, NJ, 1927: 3 (top, bottom), 9, 20, 32, 67

"Birds Eye Cook Book," Frosted Foods Sales Corp., New York, NY, 1941: jacket, 4, 68 (bottom), 70 (top, bottom), 71 (top, bottom), 78, 79

"Borden's Eagle Brand Book of Recipes," The Borden Company, New York, NY, undated: cover (two images), contents (two images), 26, 34

"Borden's Evaporated Milk," The Borden Company, New York, NY, undated: xvi, 64, 74, 82, 90, back jacket

"Cake Secrets," Swans Down Cake Flour, Igleheart Bros., 1919: cover (three images), contents, 95 (two images), 96, 101

"Canning, Preserving & Jelly Making," The Aluminum Cooking Utensil Co., New Kensington, PA, undated: xxvi

"Ceresota Cook Book," The Northwestern Consolidated Milling Co., Minneapolis, MN, undated: 30

"Cocoa and Chocolate," Walter Baker & Co., Ltd., Dorchester, MA, 1917: 97

"Dainty Desserts for Dainty People," Charles B. Knox, Johnstown, NY, 1901: 118

"Delicious Desserts and Candies," Price Flavoring Extract Co., Chicago, IL, 1923: xxxi

"Delicious Dutch Oven Dishes," Griswold Manufacturing Co., Erie, PA, undated: 48

"The Del Monte Fruit Book," California Packing Corporation, San Francisco, CA., 1926: jacket, xxviii (top), xxxi

"Experts Book on Better Cooking (Pyrex)," Corning Glass Works, Corning, NY, 1924: 5 (top), 49, 56, 93

"Favorite Recipes of the Movie Stars," Tower Books, New York, NY, 1931: 10, 11, 33, 117

"Favorite Recipes Save Time and Money," Lydia E. Pinkham Medicine Company, Lynn, MA, undated: 37 (top, bottom), 83

"Finer Flavored Milk Dishes," Libby, McNeill & Libby, Chicago, IL, 1919: xxviii (bottom), 39

"Five Easy Receipts," Gleaner Flour, undated: 36

"Food at the Fair," Exposition Publications, Inc., New York, NY, 1939: 14, 15, 58, 87

"For the Hostess," Kelvinator, Inc., Detroit, MI, undated: opposite title, viii

"From Soup to Dessert with Minute Tapioca," Minute Tapioca Company Inc., Orange, MA., 1928: title page, 92 (top)

"From the Tropics to Your Table," Fruit Dispatch Company, New York, NY, 1926: xiv, xxxiv, xxxvii, 7

"Getting His Own Breakfast," The Shredded Wheat Company, Niagara Falls, NY, 1928: jacket, xxix

"Gold Medal Flour Cook Book," Washburn-Crosby Co., Minneapolis, MN, 1910: 84

"Good Pies Easy to Make," Merrell-Soule Co., Syracuse, NY, undated: x, xi, xxxi

"Good Things to Eat Made with Arm & Hammer Baking Soda," Church & Dwight Co., Inc., New York, NY, 1925: 109

"Good Things to Eat Made with Bread," The Fleischmann Co., New York, NY 1912: 77

"Healthful Living," The Battle Creek Food Company, Battle Creek, MI, 1933: xx-xxi (borders), xx (two images), xxii (bottom), 13, 21

"Hershey's Recipes," Hershey Chocolate Corporation, Hershey, PA, 1940: jacket, borders 1-118, 104, 105

"How To Make Rennet-Custards and Ice Cream," Chr. Hansen's Laboratory, Inc., Little Falls, NY, 1938: 73, 113

"How to Serve and How to Buy Canned Salmon," Libby's Foods, 1938: jacket, 68

"Japan Tea," The Tea Exporters Association of Shizouka, undated: xxvii

"Jell-O Ice Cream Powder," The Jell-O Company, LeRoy, NY, 1925: xviii (top), xix (bottom), 22, 28

"Kate Smith's Favorite Recipes," General Foods Corporation, 1939: 99 (top, bottom)

"Kerr Home Canning Book, Kerr Glass Manufacturing Corp.," Sand Springs, OK, 1934: xxiv, xxv, 17, 72, 81 (bottom), 89, 117 (top two images)

"The Kingdom That Grew Out of a Little Boy's Garden," Hawaiian Pineapple Company, Honolulu, HI, 1931: 18 (top, bottom), 52

"Madonna Brand Recipe Booklet," Riverbank Canning Company, Riverbank, CA, undated: 50, 51

"Magic Yeast Recipes," Northwestern Yeast Co., Chicago, IL, undated: xii (three side images), 31 (top, bottom), 38 (bottom)

"McNess' Cook Book," Furst-McNess Company, Freeport, IL, undated: xxxii

"Meat: Selection, Preparation, and Many Ways to Serve," Armour and Company, Chicago, IL, 1934: 12

"Menu Magic in a Nutshell," California Walnut Growers Association, Los Angeles, CA., undated: cover, contents, 63, 103

"Modern Menus and Recipes for Your Health," Battle Creek Health Foods, Battle Creek, MI, undated: xxii (top), 23

"Monarch Cook Book," Malleable Iron Range, Co., Beaver Dam, WI, undated: xi, xiii

"Nestles Everyday Recipes," Nestles Food Company, New York, NY, undated: ix (three images), xxx

"New Party Cakes," Gold Medal Foods, Inc., General Mills, Inc., Minneapolis, MN 1931: 98

"The Recipe Book for Club," The Club Aluminum Co., Yonkers, NY, undated: 8, 46, 62, 75, 80

"Reliable Recipes," Calumet Baking Powder, Chicago, IL, undated: 100

"The Silent Hostess Treasure Book," General Electric Company, Cleveland, OH, 1930: xii, xv (three images), xxxv, 5 (bottom), 6, 44, 81 (top), 110

"Sixty-five Delicious Dishes Made with Bread," The Fleischmann Co., New York, NY, 1919: 76

"60 Ways to Serve Ham," Armour and Company, Chicago, IL; undated: cover (three images), half-title, contents, 11, 45 (top, bottom), 54 (top, bottom), 57

"Soups, Salads, and Desserts," The Burt Olney Canning Co., Oneida, NY, 1909: 24

"Stretching Meat," General Mills Inc., undated: 55, 59, 65

"The Sunday American Cook Book," The Boston Sunday American, Boston, MA, 1911: 60

"Sunkist Recipes," California Fruit Growers Exchange, Los Angeles, CA., 1916: jacket, 42, 43 (top, bottom), 72 (top)

"Tappan Cook Book," The Tappan Stove Co., Mansfield, OH, undated: x

"Tempting Davis Recipes," The Davis Baking Powder Company, Hoboken, NJ, 1925: xxx

"Thirty-three Select Recipes," Ceresota Flour, The Northwestern Consolidated Milling Co., Minneapolis, MN, 1933: cover, 38, 40, 106

"200 Tested Recipes," The Proctor & Gamble Co., Cincinnati, OH, undated: xxxvi

"WFBL Cook Book of the Stars," Onondaga Radio Broadcasting Corp., Syracuse, NY, 1945: 51

"Watkins Extract Book," The J.R. Watkins Medical Company: 29

Bibliography

Claiborne, Craig, *The New York Times Food Encyclopedia*, Times Books, 1985.

Cowan, Ruth Schwartz, *More Work for Mother: The Ironies of Household Technology from the Open Hearth to the Microwave*, Basic Books, Inc., 1983.

Hale, William Harlan, *The Horizon Cookbook and Illustrated History of Eating and Drinking through the Ages*, American Heritage, 1968.

Jones, Evan, *American Food: The Gastronomic Story*, E. P. Dutton, 1975.

Levenstein, Harvey, *Revolution at the Table*, Oxford University Press, 1988.

Mariani, John F., *The Dictionary of American Food*, Hearst Books, 1994.

Plante, Ellen M., *The American Kitchen 1700 to the Present: From Hearth to Highrise*, Facts on File, 1995.

Root, Waverly, *Food*, Simon and Schuster, 1980.

Shapiro, Laura, *Perfection Salad: Women and Cooking at the Turn of the Century*, Farrar, Straus and Giroux, 1986.

Trager, James, *The Enriched Fortified Concentrated Country-Fresh Lip-Smacking Finger-Licking International Unexpurgated Foodbook*, Grossman Publishers, 1970.

Trager, James, *The Food Chronology*, Henry Holt, 1995.

Wason, Betty, *Cooks, Gluttons and Gourmets*, Doubleday & Company Inc., 1962.

Index

A
"A Jell-O Year," 110–11
"Adventures in Corn Meal Cookery" (Quaker Corn Meal), 40–41, 106
advertising, xxviii–xxxi
"Aladdin's Lamp at Mealtimes" (Premier Pure Food Products), 23
Allen, Gracie, 53
"American Cookery," 104
Anne of Austria, 96
apples, 98, 102
"Arm & Hammer Book of Valuable Recipes," 7
asparagus, 23
avocados, 6, 10
"Ayer's Preserve Book," 29

B
Baked Carrots and Potatoes, 82
Baked Fish with Mustard Sauce, 64–65
Baked Pork Chops with Apples, 54
Baked Round of Beef with Horseradish, 46–47
Baked Spring Chicken, 60–61
Baked Tomatoes, 86
baking powder, 38
Baltimore Crab Cakes, 67
Banana Waffles, 34–35
bananas, xxxviii, 34–35
"Bananas in the Modern Manner," 34–35
Battle Creek Sanitarium, xxi–xxii
beans, black, 87
beans, cacao, 96–97
beans, kidney, xxxv
beans, navy, 18–19, 56
beans, wax, 24
Beard, James, 4, 62
"Beardsley's Helpful Suggestions," 20
beef, 46–53
Beet Aspic, 22
beets, 22
Bermuda Relish Canapés, 4
Berry Cream, 115

Birdseye, Clarence, 78
"Birds Eye Cook Book," 70–71, 78–79
Bittersweet Chocolate Jewel Cake, 96–97
Black Beans Havana—Frijoles Negros, 87
blandness of food, xxxiii, xxxv, 16, 48–49
"Book of Recipes" (Borden's), 74–75
Borden, Gail, xiv–xvii, 82
"Boston Cooking School Cook Book," xxvi–xxvii
bread, 30–43
"Bread: The Most Important of All Foods" (Spaulding's Blue Ribbon Bread), 32
bread pudding, 108–109
Brewster Asparagus Salad, 23
Bunny Sausage, 58
Burns, George, 53
butter, xxv, 47
Butterscotch Curls, 36

C
"Cake Secrets" (Swans Down), 95
cakes, 95–101
canapés, 4–5
canned foods, xi, xxiii, xxvii–xxviii, 117
"Carnation Cook Book," 82, 88–89
carrots, 82, 92
caviar, 25
cheese, 74–75
cheese cake, 99
Cheese Canapés, 5
"Cheese Recipes" (Baumert Cheese), 4–5
chicken, 58–61
Chicken Patties, 58
chili, xxxv
chocolate, 96–97, 104–105, 108, 116
Chocolate Bittersweet Cookies, 104–105
Chocolate Bread Pudding, 108–109

chocolate mousse, 116
Church, James A., 38
cinnamon, 32
Cinnamon Toast, 32
"Cocoa and Chocolate," 97, 104
cole slaw, 26
"Complete Cottage Cheese Recipe Book, The" (Pennsupreme), 99
condensed milk, xv, 82
condensed soup, xxiii
"Cook Book and Facts Worth Knowing" (Cow Brand soda), 102
"Cook Book of the Stars, The," 18–19, 37, 50–51, 53
Cooke, Mrs. John E., 26
cookies, 104–107
Cooper, Gary, 33
corn, 40, 83, 106
Corn Meal Cookies, 106
crab cakes, 67
cream cheese, 4, 7
Cream of Onion Soup, 12
Crisco, xxv
croquettes, 66–67
Cucumber Mayonnaise, 73
curry powder, 16, 68

D
"Dainty Desserts for Dainty People" (Knox Gelatin), 118
Date and Nut Bread, 39
dates, 39
Dauviller, Jules, 8
desserts, 94–119
"Dining Delights" (Colman's Mustard), 67
Dutch Apple Cake, 98

E
Edward R. Murrow's Oatmeal Scones, 37
electric ranges, xiii
electric refrigerators, xiv–xv, xxxv
Escalloped Corn, 83
Escalloped Macaroni with Cheese, 74–75
evaporated milk, xvii, 82, 91

Old-Time Brand-Name Desserts

Old-Time Brand-Name Desserts

Recipes, Illustrations, and Advice
from the Recipe Pamphlets of America's
Most Trusted Food Makers

B U N N Y C R U M P A C K E R

ABRADALE PRESS
HARRY N. ABRAMS, INC., PUBLISHERS

Acknowledgments

For enthusiastic recipe testing, great thanks to Jody Richards, who swims in the Hudson River, and to Lynda Johnson, on an island in Puget Sound. My thanks too to testers Cassidy Cokeley and Louise Rogers. I'm very grateful to two Joannes, both of whom lent me books: JoAnn Shaheen, for her grandmother's copy of "The Monarch Iron Range Book," and Joanne Rubin, who sent "More Work for Mother." Love and thanks to Chick and Casey Crumpacker, who tasted *everything*.

BLUE LABEL MENUS

Contents

ost of us look forward to dessert. It's taken into consideration well before it occurs. After all, dessert is not casual. It doesn't just happen. The right dessert involves choice and planning and imagination and hope. If a good meal were a story, dessert would be the last word, the "amen." Dessert concludes, it punctuates, it's the exclamation point,

the period. Dessert is a coda, a full stop, a happy ending. Dessert is the taste you're left with, and it's the first memory of a meal you've already eaten.

There are people who eat dessert for the same reason

other people climb a mountain: because it's there. There are others, sweet souls, who see beyond the obvious. They recognize dessert for what it is — a dream, a delight, a virtue, a reward. I ate my vegetables; now, I want my dessert. *Give me my dessert!*

Into which category do I fall? For a long time, in restaurants, given a menu, I'd choose dessert first. Then I'd plan the rest of the meal. Now, I'm more moderate. I choose the appetizer first; *then* I decide on dessert. The middle either falls into place or it can be dispensed with altogether. This is a menu philosophy that goes with the T-shirt advice, "Life is short. Eat dessert first."

Desserts are made with just a few basic ingredients: sugar (the *sine qua non*), butter, flour, milk, flavoring, and perhaps some fruit. If it seems strange that these precious few ingredients can be combined and recombined to create so many wonderful and different desserts, consider that just the twenty-six letters of the alphabet are enough for both Shakespeare *and* the Marx Brothers, and only ten digits are enough to count everything in the universe.

Aside from cholesterol and the sugar blues (a small worry if one can manage to eat in moderation), desserts can be close to perfect. But even so, cooking is not about perfection. Cooking is about imagination, taste, history, tradition, spirit, and, when you're lucky, love. It surely would be a sadder world without the sweetness of dessert.

From Yesterday's Kitchens

All the recipes in this book, like those in my first book, *The Old-Time Brand-Name Cookbook,* are based on cooking pamphlets issued by food manufacturers in the years from 1875 to 1950. The time span encompassed by these recipe pamphlets begins with the late Industrial Revolution, and reaches to the beginnings of the truly modern kitchen, just after World War II. At the beginning of that three-generation span, the first processed foods were introduced. Such products of the Industrial Revolution as packaged yeast, powdered gelatin, and baking powder are foods we take for granted today. We don't even think of them as processed, though they are.

For cooks in the last quarter of the nineteenth century, those first processed foods were miracles of convenience and speed. Before then, cooking was incredibly tedious and time-consuming. In order to make something as simple as a gelatin dessert, for instance, long hours had to be spent boiling beef and veal bones for a stock sufficiently strong and reduced to gel. There were no refrigerators, no gas or electric stoves, no canned or frozen foods. The beef bones for gelatin were cooked over an iron range that burned wood or coal — and that in itself was an advance from cooking over an open hearth.

In order to heat the iron stove, the cook had to shovel out the cold ashes, build a new fire, replenish it, and guess at the temperature (by holding her hand in the oven, or, as one household hint of the day had it, by putting a piece of paper in the oven and noting how quickly it turned brown and began to burn). Once the right temperature (or thereabouts) was reached, it had to be maintained, and when all the cooking was done and the stove was cold, the cook had to polish it with blacking to make it clean again. And before she cooked another meal, she had to go out and chop the wood — or shovel the coal — for the next fire. It is with good reason that Charles Dickens called the first cast-iron stoves red-hot monsters.

Similarly, the ice box was an advance over the cold cellar: It was a convenience but it still meant enormous amounts of work. Ice had to be delivered with some frequency, and when it melted, the drip-pan had to be emptied promptly. The inside of the ice box wasn't very large, but it meant that for the first time food could be kept without spoiling. Rot and decay, the old enemies of breakfast, lunch, and dinner, were not routed, but they had suffered a significant defeat.

In those nineteenth-century kitchens, where so much work was devoted simply to *getting ready* to cook, and then to recovering from the meal and restoring the kitchen to order, nearly every family had help in the kitchen. All the household chores — cooking and cleaning and sewing and washing and ironing and mending and keeping a kitchen garden and going to market for the things you couldn't grow, plus taking care of the children — all this was enormously cumbersome and each activity meant hours of work. A girl in the kitchen was the norm for those who could afford her. A whole battery of servants worked in the big houses on the hill.

The Industrial Revolution changed all that. Servants left the kitchens they worked in because work in the factories paid better, the hours were shorter and more regular, and working in a factory was a step up from being a servant in someone else's house. Back in the kitchen, alone for the first time, women suddenly were faced with preparing three meals a day, and some of them didn't even know how to cook. They were saved, though, and by the same factories that had taken away their helpers, because the new factories manufactured the products — the first processed foods — that were to make

"YOU MAY TAKE THIS MENU BOOK AND MAKE UP A CURTICE DINNER TO-DAY!"

life in the kitchen easier and simpler. The gelatin that once had to be boiled for hours now came in boxes, powdered and flavored; all you had to do was add hot water and sugar and stir. Presto! Put the result in the ice box, or, soon, the electric refrigerator, and dessert was ready.

New products came tumbling out of the factories one after another. There were packages of ground tapioca and individually wrapped cakes of yeast. There was baking powder in tins. There were bottles of molasses and cans of evaporated milk. There were packages of sugar, vegetable shortening and presliced bread, bags of flour, and cooking chocolate. There were little bottles of flavoring extracts and the appearance of the almost miraculous canned foods. Canned foods, as luck would have it, were produced before there were can openers (there wasn't any point in having an opener without a can) and for a little while the best way to open a can of peaches was with a hatchet.

There were new foods too, exotic things like bananas and oranges and pineapples and avocados. There is a reason why good children found oranges in their

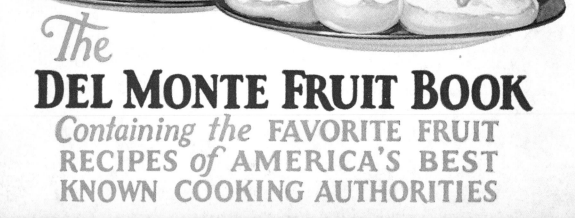

The
DEL MONTE FRUIT BOOK
Containing the FAVORITE FRUIT RECIPES of AMERICA'S BEST KNOWN COOKING AUTHORITIES

Suit the *color* to the use
(3 easy rules)

TIPPED WITH GREEN? It's partially ripe. Cook it! The pulp is firm, starchy, slightly tart ... just right to cook and serve with the main course as a vegetable.

ALL YELLOW? It's yellow-ripe, when the green has disappeared from the tip ... ready to eat or cook ... excellent for pies, cakes, puddings and waffles, muffins and bread.

FLECKED WITH BROWN? Now it's fully ripe ... in its golden prime, the best stage for eating! It's sweet, mellow ... thoroughly digestible and just right for fruit cups, salads, desserts and drinks.

stockings on Christmas morning. Oranges were rare and wonderful. Santa brought them all the way from the tropics, undoubtedly cooling them at the North Pole. It was *all* awesome once — the gas stove that you turned on with little handles, the refrigerator with its art deco coil on the top, the packages with their beautiful lettering on the outside and amazing ingredients on the inside.

Women had to learn how to use these new processed and exotic foods. That was the first point of the early recipe pamphlets. Some of them focused on a single product: a pamphlet on baking cakes distributed by a flour or baking powder manufacturer like Hecker's, Rumford, or Calumet, chocolate recipes from Hershey or Baker's, gelatin desserts from Knox and Jell-O. Others were complete cookbooks, with recipes for everything, and household hints as well. Some of the all-purpose pamphlets had holes in one corner and a loop of cord threaded through the hole, presumably for hanging from a kitchen hook.

There were food adventurers behind the products and the pamphlets. They were people with vision and tenacity who took their ideas and dreams and made them real. Charles Fleischmann peddled yeast door to door and Richard Hellman figured out how to bottle his mayonnaise. Charles Knox watched his wife boil bones for gelatin and thought there must be a better way. Milton Snaveley Hershey borrowed money from his aunt so he could figure out how to coat his caramels with chocolate.

Borden's Evaporated Milk Book of Recipes

The now-familiar product names belonged to real people like these and Gail Borden, James Kraft, Clarence Birdseye, and John Harvey Kellogg, among many others.

Once, we ate what we grew: rhubarb in the spring, strawberries in June, tomatoes in August, apples in the autumn, and cider in the winter. In order to have milk, you either kept a cow or you knew someone who did. Meat was pork, because pork could be preserved. When the pig was slaughtered, there was fresh meat. Other times, families ate ham and bacon, and used lard and salt pork for cooking. There were only a few foods that had to be purchased: sugar (though some families made their own sorghum and others boiled sap to make maple syrup), flour, salt, pepper, and such occasional treats as raisins and chocolate.

The food business then meant growing food, transporting it, and selling it to a hungry market. But with the onset of the Industrial Revolution and the new processed foods, the consumer suddenly had to be convinced to buy *this* kind of food rather than that, and *this* brand, not that. Before, it was a question of filling a demand. Now, a demand had to be *created.* Suddenly, the consumer had

HEALTHFUL LIVING

FUNDAMENTAL FACTS ABOUT FOOD AND FEEDING

choices. The pamphlets were part of that process, just as they were part of teaching women how to use the new foods. In a way, they led to the first liberation of women from the endless work of the kitchen.

The pamphlets were also part of the food trends that followed one another in succession. One of the first was for "scientific" food, food that had more to do with morality, chemistry, and a view of the rational than it did with taste. "Dainty" food looked cute and neat and helped to disassociate food on the plate from the messy reality of the kitchen. There was glamorous food, like the movie stars ate. There was food that once it was inside would keep families safe from almost any disaster — a barricade against unhappiness as well as against germs. Perhaps best of all, cooking was a way to win love — first for "Little Miss Bride" and later, for long-suffering mother.

Just after World War II, a wave of international food began, with pizza and chop suey replacing the bland innocence of chili made without chili powder or cumin or hot peppers, and curries made with a quarter teaspoon of curry powder. The tide of white sauce that had long covered our nation's plates from coast to coast began to ebb, and herbs and spices — a new world beyond salt and pepper — began to appear in lists of recipe ingredients.

Today, strawberries and asparagus are available all year around — fresh, frozen, or canned — and dozens of varieties of rice, cereal, and mustard are on supermarket shelves in cities and towns everywhere. We have freezers and microwaves, and we can zap a cup of soup, a meal, or a bowl of popcorn in mere seconds.

The old pamphlets, each one filled with its own kind of excitement and awe about its marvelous product, tell us about our past as it was reflected by food. They are a translation into food, in recipes and glowing art, of our history. Their recipes, adapted for both *The Old-Time Brand-Name Cookbook* and *Old-Time Brand-Name Desserts*, tell us what our grandparents and their parents ate for breakfast, lunch, and dinner. They are our kitchen heritage, and they still taste wonderful.

*L*eft-over pieces of plain cake or cookies may be heated carefully in a steamer, and served with sweet pudding sauce. . . .

Or they may be steamed and put into a dish covered with a boiled custard, and a meringue and served cold.

Or they may be covered with hot stewed berries or other fruit, sufficient to moisten, and served with cream.

Cakes

Or they may be used in place of bread crumbs in scalloped apple, fruit charlotte, or bread or cabinet pudding.

Stale sponge cake may be used as above, or to line a mould, or to serve as a foundation for whipped cream.

Left Overs or Economy in the Kitchen, War Edition, C. I. Hood;
Hood's Sarsaparilla, c. 1918

Banana Upside-Down Cake
(and Banana Whipped Cream Cake)

*I*n the nineteenth century, bananas were exotic fruit. Workers in the tropical fields where they grew were beset by yellow fever, malaria, and dysentery. Shippers depended on calm seas for fast voyages, and bananas were shipped only in the spring, summer, and fall, because they'd freeze aboard ship in the winter. In 1870, the Cape Cod schooner *Telegraph* picked up 160 bunches of Jamaican bananas. The captain had tried bananas and liked them and when he saw the bunches on the pier while he was loading other cargo, he decided to try bringing them back to the United States. They were still green,

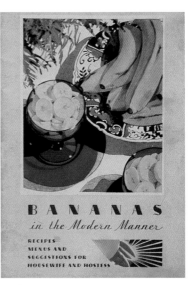

and the seller told him he had 14 days before they'd spoil. The weather was good; he made it to Jersey City in two weeks, and he sold his bananas — now yellow — at a profit of $2 a bunch. The next schooner load brought bananas to Boston. Nearly 30 years later, in 1899, Boston Fruit merged with United Fruit and bananas began arriving regularly at American ports.

1 large egg	1 teaspoon cream of tartar
2 tablespoons melted unsalted butter	1 cup sugar
plus 1/2 cup unsalted butter, melted	1/2 teaspoon salt
(see notes)	1 teaspoon pure lemon extract
milk	3/4 cup brown sugar, loosely packed
1 1/2 cups flour	3 bananas, peeled and sliced
1/2 teaspoon baking soda (see notes)	

1. Preheat the oven to 325 degrees.
2. Break the egg into a 1-cup measuring cup. Add the 2 tablespoons melted butter and then fill the cup with milk. Turn into a mixing bowl and beat lightly. In a separate bowl, mix together the flour, baking soda, cream of tartar, sugar, and salt. Gradually add the dry

mixture to the milk mixture, stirring to combine thoroughly. Add the lemon extract and beat until creamy.

3. Pour the remaining ½ cup melted butter into an 8-inch square baking pan. Spread the brown sugar over the bottom of the pan and then arrange the sliced bananas over the sugar. Pour the batter over the bananas.

4. Bake for 30 minutes, or until golden brown and a toothpick poked into the center of the cake comes out clean. Cool in the pan. Either turn the cake out onto a platter so that the bananas are on top, making a true upside-down cake, or make life a little easier for yourself and serve directly from the baking pan.

Notes: For this cake, butter is measured two ways: first, by spooning out 2 tablespoons of butter that has already been melted, and next by measuring ½ cup butter and *then* melting it. You can substitute 1½ teaspoons baking powder for the baking soda and cream of tartar. Finally, the cake is particularly lovely, as is almost everything, served with whipped cream.

8 to 10 servings

Adapted from "Bananas in the Modern Manner"
Banana Growers Association, 1930

Variation:

Banana Whipped Cream Cake

Make the batter for Banana Upside-Down Cake and bake it in two buttered 8-inch cake pans at 325 degrees for 30 minutes, or until golden brown and a toothpick poked into the center of the cakes comes out clean. Cool the layers on a rack. Whip 1 cup heavy cream until it's thick; sweeten with 1 tablespoon sugar and add ½ teaspoon pure vanilla extract. Place the bottom cake layer on a serving plate; cover with slices of ripe banana and spread with half the whipped cream. Place the second layer on top and heap with more bananas and the remaining whipped cream. Garnish, if you like, with a sprinkle of walnuts. Adapted from "From the Tropics to Your Table," Fruit Dispatch Company, published in 1926.

Apple Butter Refrigerator Roll

Apple Butter Refrigerator Roll sounds very fancy, but all it is at heart is a variation of the kind of dessert Girl Scouts love to make. Mind you, that doesn't diminish it one whit. Think of s'mores or Samoas or thin mint cookies: delicious then, delicious now. Teenagers often learn to cook by following an almost magical recipe for chocolate wafers sandwiched with whipped cream and left to soften into a creamy, chocolatey whole. Here, we have a grown-up variation. A favorite of mine is made with thin ginger snaps, whipped cream, and chopped crystallized ginger and the same process. At the end, I add blueberries on top. None of these recipes is adolescent. Just delectable.

1 cup heavy cream
⅓ cup apple butter (see note)

30 vanilla wafers, the thinnest you can find
chopped nuts (optional)

1. Whip the cream until it holds soft peaks. Gradually add the apple butter and continue to beat until the cream holds firm peaks.
2. Spread whipped cream mixture on one side of a wafer, top with another wafer, and spread more whipped cream on the second wafer. Stand the wafers on edge on a serving dish, and continue to add wafers and whipped cream, forming a long roll. (If your serving dish isn't large enough, make your roll two wafers wide rather than one.) When all the wafers are used, spread the remaining whipped cream mixture on the top and sides of the roll. If you like, garnish the top with chopped nuts.
3. Chill for at least 3 hours. To serve, slice diagonally across the roll.

Note: If you'd rather use another flavor of preserves, including sugar-free jam, by all means do.

6 servings

Adapted from "Recipe Book"
Heinz, 1939

Busy Mother's Cake

Before World War II , most mothers didn't have jobs outside the home. But *inside* the home, they had to boil their baby's cloth diapers, handwash the laundry and hang it on the clothesline to dry, go food shopping daily at the grocer's and the butcher's, prepare a hot lunch for the family, defrost the refrigerator monthly, and, as they say, much more. There were no supermarkets, freezers, washing machines, driers, or dishwashers. There was just Mom. And along with everything else, Mom was expected to make her own desserts. And there were no cake mixes. General Mills and Pillsbury didn't introduce their mixes, in just three flavors (or colors, if you prefer) — chocolate, gold, and white — until 1948. Duncan Hines followed in 1951 with a single mix that made a white cake if you added egg white, a yellow cake if you added a whole egg, or a chocolate cake if you added an egg and cocoa. In those days, a cake for busy mothers (the butter doesn't have to be creamed) was an enticement. It still is.

1/4 cup melted unsalted butter plus butter for the pan	4 tablespoons water
	1 teaspoon pure vanilla extract
3 eggs	1 cup flour
1 cup sugar	1 teaspoon baking powder

1. Preheat the oven to 325 degrees. Butter an 8-inch square baking pan, two 9-inch layer cake pans, *or* two six-muffin tins.

2. Beat the eggs in a bowl until they are slightly thickened and pale yellow. Gradually beat in the sugar. Add the water and vanilla, and mix well.

3. Mix the flour and baking powder in a separate bowl and fold this mixture into the egg batter. Fold in the melted butter.

4. Pour the batter into the buttered baking pan, layer cake pans, or muffin tins.

5. Bake for 40 minutes if you are using the square dish, 30 minutes for the layer cake pans, or 20 minutes for the muffin tins. The cake is done when a toothpick poked into the center comes out clean.

10 to 12 servings

Adapted from "Requested Recipes"
New York Daily News, 1940

Devil's Food Cake

The Baker's Chocolate pamphlet that this recipe comes from tells us that chocolate is "a beneficent restorer of exhausted power," and that it's good for public speakers and "all those who give to work a portion of the time needed for sleep." And because it soothes both stomach and brain, "it is the best friend of those engaged in literary pursuits."

A literary pursuit of a poetic kind must have been involved in the naming of Devil's Food Cake. Was it so named because it's a cake so deeply chocolatey, rich, and delicious that it must be sinful? Not like Angel Food Cake, which is dry, snowy, and very pale. Angel Food Cake is what you do with leftover egg whites, and it has been around since the 1870s. Devil's Food Cake uses whole eggs, and it appeared later, just after the turn of the century. Were we more wicked then? First Paradise and then the Fall? To consider these questions, it might be wise to have a piece of devilishly good Devil's Food Cake and engage in some literary pursuits of your own.

½ cup unsalted butter at room temperature
  plus butter for the cake pans

3 squares (3 ounces) unsweetened chocolate

2 cups cake flour

1 teaspoon baking soda

2 cups sifted brown sugar, loosely packed

2 eggs

1¼ cups buttermilk

1 teaspoon pure vanilla extract

1. Butter two 8-inch cake pans.
2. Preheat the oven to 325 degrees and as the oven heats up, melt the chocolate in a dry pan, watching it carefully; it will soften in a very few minutes. Remove the pan from the oven and allow to cool slightly. In a small bowl, combine the cake flour and the baking soda. Set aside.
3. Cream the butter, and gradually add the brown sugar, continuing to beat until the mixture is light and fluffy. Add the eggs, one at a time, beating thoroughly after each. Add the chocolate, and mix well. Alternately and by thirds, add the flour mixture and the buttermilk, beginning and ending with flour and beating after each addition until smooth. Add the vanilla and mix again. Divide the batter between the buttered cake pans.
4. Bake for 35 minutes, or until a toothpick poked into the center of the cakes comes out clean.

Here we have the beginning and ending of two fables, one happy and one sad. The first "Little Bride" made her husband's birthday cake the right way: she used Gold Medal flour and a

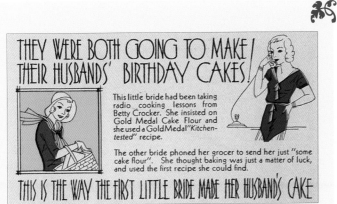

Gold Medal recipe. And her husband loved her for it. The other husband — "poor chap" — was presented with a messy, gloppy looking cake, made with any old flour, and could barely choke down a few bites. Thus does baking become a moral force: the second marriage is obviously doomed, unless the Little Bride learns more about brand names. To me, though the second bride looks a bit more like a free spirit — her husband is her main problem. And the first marriage is just a bit too perfect. Look at their faces! You know right away you don't want to invite them over for dinner. Will they live happily ever after — just Mr. and Mrs. Perfect and their beautiful cake? Don't count on it.

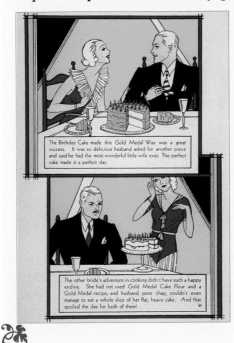

Note: Frost, or serve with whipped cream or ice cream. There are some who serve a piece of cake with a scoop of ice cream and top it off with chocolate sauce. Talk about devilish!

8 to 10 servings

Adapted from "Chocolate Cookery"
Baker's Chocolate, 1929

Mrs. Hammer's Cheese Cake

Cheesecake has a long and honorable pedigree. It was one of the earliest printed recipes: The Roman statesman Cato the Elder included in his writings a recipe for a ricotta cheesecake made with honey. But I'm sure cheesecake goes back even further, to the moment when someone noticed that curd cheese tasted wonderful mixed with something sweet. Smooth cheesecakes came long after Cato's noble Roman ricotta cheesecake. Best known of the smooth cheesecakes is what's known as New York cheesecake, made famous by Lindy's and made frozen by Sara Lee.

Smooth cheesecake was cooked for the first time in the last third of the nineteenth century, when cream cheese was developed in upstate New York. At first, cream cheese was made by the Empire Cheese Company. When its factory burned down, a group of farmers bought the company and reopened it as the Phenix Cheese Company, in honor of the phoenix (which they spelled wrong), the mythical bird that rose from ashes to live again. Phenix was bought by Joseph Kraft, who didn't come from upstate New York and thus named *his* product Philadelphia Cream Cheese.

But who was Mrs. Hammer? She was a woman who made good cheesecake.

2 tablespoons unsalted butter, melted,
  plus butter for the pan
14 slices zwieback, crushed (see note)
2 tablespoons sugar plus 1 cup
1 teaspoon cinnamon
1½ pounds pot or cottage cheese
  (see note)
4 eggs

1 teaspoon lemon juice
grated rind of 1 lemon
1 tablespoon flour
1 cup heavy cream, or, if using cottage
  cheese, ³⁄₄ cup
8 ounces crushed pineapple in its own
  juice, well drained (optional)

1. Preheat the oven to 350 degrees. Butter an 8-inch springform pan or an 8-inch square baking pan.
2. Crush the zwieback by pulsing in a food processor or by placing zwieback between two sheets of wax paper and crushing with a rolling pin. Mix the crumbs with 2 tablespoons

sugar, the cinnamon, and melted butter. Reserve ¼ cup of this mixture. Pat the remaining mixture over the sides and bottom of the buttered pan. Set aside.

3. If you have a food processor, combine the pot cheese with the eggs, adding them one at a time, and pulsing each into the cheese. Otherwise, in a large mixing bowl, combine the cheese with the eggs, adding them one at a time. Add the lemon juice and rind, the remaining 1 cup of sugar, and the flour, pulsing several times, or mixing well. Blend in the cream. (Be sure to use only ¾ cup of cream if you're using cottage rather than pot cheese.)

4. Scatter the pineapple, if using, over the crumbs in the baking pan. Pour in the cheese batter and sprinkle the reserved crumbs over the top.

5. Bake for 1 hour, or until firm in the center. Turn off the heat but leave the cake in the oven, with the door propped slightly open, until it is no longer hot. Then remove it and allow it to cool to room temperature. If you're using the springform pan, run a knife between the sides of the form and the cake and then remove the pan's sides. If you're using the square baking pan, serve the cake directly from the pan. Refrigerate to keep.

Note: Zwieback is a rectangular piece of bread that has been slowly toasted until it's dry and hard. You can find zwieback in the cookie section of your supermarket; if it's not there, look among the baby foods — it's a good, chewy snack for teething babies. Pot cheese is usually available in the cottage cheese section of the dairy case at your supermarket.

10 servings

Adapted from "Requested Recipes"
New York Daily News, 1940

Dutch Crumb Cake

A very refined crumb cake is this — no mile-high coating of crumbs, just a discreet topping of butter, brown sugar, and flour. It is quiet and unassuming, by nature tender and delicate, sweet, but with a slight hint of buttermilk's tang. In short, it's delectable.

2½ cups cake flour
½ teaspoon salt
½ teaspoon baking soda
½ cup unsalted butter at room temperature
   plus butter for the pan
1½ cups brown sugar, lightly packed
1 cup raisins (optional)
1 egg, lightly beaten
¾ cup buttermilk
2 tablespoons granulated sugar
¼ teaspoon cinnamon

1. Preheat the oven to 350 degrees. Butter an 8-inch square baking pan.
2. Combine the flour, salt, and baking soda. Set aside.
3. Cream the butter thoroughly. Gradually add the brown sugar and continue beating until light and fluffy. Stir in the flour. Remove ¾ cup of this mixture and reserve it.
4. Add the raisins, if using, to the remaining butter and sugar mixture. Add the egg and buttermilk and beat well.
5. Pour the batter (which is fairly thick) into the buttered pan, levelling the top with a spatula. Sprinkle the reserved butter and flour mixture over the batter. Combine the granulated sugar and cinnamon and sprinkle on top of the butter and flour mixture.
6. Bake for 30 to 40 minutes, until lightly browned and a toothpick poked into the cake comes out clean.

10 to 12 servings

Adapted from "Home Baked Delicacies"
Swans Down, 1929

Ersatz (or Quick) Dobos Torte

Ersatz (or Quick) Dobos Torte is a wonderfully elaborate and delicious variation of pound cake. *Ersatz* is a German word meaning not the real thing; in this case, the real thing would take a whole lot longer to produce. The ersatz cake starts with an already baked pound cake.

The recipe is from a pamphlet published during the heyday of American railroads, when the Santa Fe Railway's signature train, the Super Chief, brought excellent service to the Southwest. Many of its stops were just for eating at Harvey House restaurants. When the train had a dining car, Harvey House also supplied meals on board and, let it be noted, served 1,100 pounds of this cake every year. The recipe was one of the most requested by passengers, and was published in the "Super Chief Cook Book," which notes that it is ersatz because the special baking pans needed to make a real Dobos Torte are not always available to home bakers. It's an elegant extravaganza, ersatz or otherwise.

1 pound cake, fresh or frozen
1⅓ cups semisweet chocolate chips
⅔ cup heavy cream
½ pound sweet chocolate

1. Trim the crusts from the cake. Cut the cake in half lengthwise, and slice each half into 6 or 8 very thin slices, parallel to the top.
2. Melt the chocolate chips in a double boiler over hot water; remove from the heat and let cool.
3. Whip the cream until it holds firm peaks. Fold the cooled chocolate into the whipped cream.
4. Spread the chocolate cream between the slices of each half cake, placing each slice on top of the one before.
5. Melt the sweet chocolate in a clean, dry double boiler over hot water. Cool slightly and pour over the top and sides of the cakes to make a thin coating. Chill until firm. Slice and serve.

2 cakes, or 16 servings

Adapted from "Super Chief Cook Book of Famous Fred Harvey Recipes"
Santa Fe Railway and Fred Harvey Restaurants, undated

Lady Goldenglow Second Mystery Cake

What a name! Who could resist it? This cake joins the tiny ranks of noble cakes, best known of which is Lady Baltimore Cake made with egg whites, and Lord Baltimore Cake made with yolks — something like Jack Sprat and the missus of Mother Goose fame.

Perhaps the cake is called Goldenglow because half of it is made with orange extract. And maybe the Mystery is because it's marbled: How do they do that? (It's really simple, just a spoonful of this followed by a spoonful of that.) The *Second* mystery is probably because there's a *First* Mystery Cake. It has a subtitle, Tropic Aroma Cake, but no Mystery. And it isn't noble, like Lady Goldenglow, which has it all.

1 cup unsalted butter at room temperature
  plus butter for the pan

2 cups sugar

4 eggs

3 cups flour

1 tablespoon baking powder

½ teaspoon salt

1 cup milk

1 teaspoon pure orange extract

1½ squares (1½ ounces) unsweetened
  chocolate, melted

1 teaspoon pure vanilla extract

ORANGE FROSTING:

½ cup unsalted butter

pinch of salt

grated zest of 1 orange

1 teaspoon pure orange extract

4 cups sifted confectioners' sugar

5 tablespoons milk or orange juice, as
  needed

ORANGE WHIPPED CREAM:

1½ cups heavy cream

4 tablespoons sugar

grated zest of 1 orange

1 teaspoon pure orange extract

sweet or bittersweet chocolate shavings
  or sprinkles (optional)

1. Preheat the oven to 325 degrees. Butter 2 layer-cake pans.
2. Cream the butter until it's soft and light. Gradually add the sugar, beating well and stopping to scrape down the sides of the bowl at least once. Add the eggs, one at a time, beating after each addition.
3. Mix the flour, baking powder, and salt in a separate bowl, and add to the batter in thirds, alternating with the milk,

beginning and ending with the flour mixture. Remove half the batter to a separate bowl. Add the orange extract to the batter remaining in the first bowl, and mix thoroughly. Add the melted chocolate and vanilla to the second bowl and mix well.

4. Divide the batter between the cake pans by tablespoons: first one of the orange mixture, then one of the chocolate, and so on. Bake for 30 to 40 minutes, or until a toothpick poked into the center of the cakes comes out clean. Cool on a rack.

5. Spread Orange Frosting or Orange Whipped Cream over one layer. Top with the second layer, and ice the top and sides with the remaining frosting or whipped cream. To garnish, sprinkle with chocolate shavings.

ORANGE FROSTING: Cream the butter with the salt, orange zest, and orange extract; gradually add the sugar and milk or orange juice, adding more milk or juice as needed to make a spreadable frosting.

ORANGE WHIPPED CREAM: Whip the cream until soft peaks form; add the sugar, grated zest, and orange extract, and beat until firm.

Note: It's also possible to use half orange and half chocolate frosting — one for the filling and one for the top. In that case, before adding the orange zest and extract to the frosting, remove half, just as you did for the cake, and add orange extract to one half and 1½ squares (1½ ounces) chocolate, melted and cooled, to the other. Use the chocolate icing as filling and the orange icing on the top and sides of the cake. You can also fill the cake with Orange Whipped Cream and ice it with Orange Frosting.

10 servings

Adapted from "Royal Cook Book"
Standard Brands, Inc., 1930

Whether one is giving an affair, or whether a friend or two drop in during the afternoon, or whether one is alone, the custom of a cup of Afternoon Tea between four and five o'clock is well worth instituting.

Make ready an afternoon tea shelf in your butler's pantry, or in a corner of your kitchen cupboard. On it assemble . . . a crystal jar filled with lemon, lime, and cinnamon drops for those who like a bit of flavor in the tea, some whole cloves for those who prefer this flavor, and one of those adorable enameled cooky boxes, which you can fill once a week with

Cookies

some old-fashioned seed cakes, hermits, or ginger drops when you do your Saturday baking . . . .

Before long you will undoubtedly find your informal Afternoon Teas growing so popular that you will wish to institute a little "At Home" every week . . . . Your simple refreshments, including the perfect tea and coffee that you will serve, and a bit of good music will soon make you famous as a hostess.

"Coffee or Tea?"
Maxwell House, undated, c. 1920

Hattie's Sugar Cookies

Cookie. The very sound of the word is sweet, playful, and innocent. *Cookie* comes from the Dutch word *koekje*, which means little cake, but there's a vast difference between a cookie and a cake. Cake is a serious thing, but cookies are pert and cute and diminutive. Cake is all grown up and well educated. Cookies are full of fun and irreverence. Cakes have icing, and layers; they get dressed up and go to weddings. Cookies stay home and eat at the children's table. The grown-ups take a cookie when they think no one is looking. Cakes are decorated, and they have decorum. Cookies are complete unto themselves and they're very easy to carry around. Hattie's Sugar Cookies are in the classic cookie mode. Like peanuts, one is too many and a thousand is not enough.

2 tablespoons unsalted butter plus butter for the cookie sheet	⅔ cup flour
½ cup sugar	1 teaspoon baking powder
1 egg, lightly beaten	pinch of salt
2 tablespoons milk	⅓ cup chopped pecans or walnuts
½ teaspoon pure vanilla extract	pecan or walnut halves (optional)

1. Preheat the oven to 375 degrees. Butter a cookie sheet.
2. Cream the butter. Gradually add the sugar, continuing to beat, stopping at least once to scrape down the sides of the bowl, until the mixture is light and fluffy. Add the egg and beat thoroughly. Add the milk and vanilla and combine.
3. Mix the flour, baking powder, and salt in a separate bowl, and stir this mixture into the creamed batter. Stir in the chopped nuts. Drop teaspoonfuls of batter about 2 inches apart onto the cookie sheet. If you like, press a nut half into the center of each cookie.
4. Bake for 10 to 12 minutes, until the cookies are a delicate brown with darker edges. Remove to a rack to cool.

Yield: 1 to 2 dozen cookies, depending on size

Adapted from "Home Cooking Album"
Wilkin Whiskey, 1935

Blueberry Drop Cookies

Blueberries all year round! That's just one of the many culinary blessings we take for granted. Still, there is nothing as good as that first mouthful of fresh, local berries — unwrapped at the sink, rinsed, and eaten by the handful. The only thing better is if you've picked them yourself and gobbled a few right then and there. Blueberries are good with cream, in pancakes, in smoothies, with cereal, in pies, cakes, and — if you hadn't considered it — in cookies as well.

½ cup unsalted butter at room temperature plus butter for the cookie sheet

1 cup sugar

1 egg, lightly beaten

½ cup milk

grated rind of ½ lemon

2½ cups flour

¼ teaspoon salt

2½ teaspoons baking powder

1 cup blueberries

1. Preheat the oven to 350 degrees. Butter a cookie sheet.

2. Cream the butter. Gradually add the sugar and mix well. Add the egg, continuing to beat.

3. In a separate bowl, combine the milk and lemon rind and, in another bowl, combine the flour, salt and baking powder. Add the milk and flour mixtures alternately to the butter, beginning and ending with the flour. Gently stir in the blueberries.

4. Drop by spoonfuls about ½ inch apart onto the buttered sheet. Bake for 12 to 15 minutes, or until lightly browned.

Yield: 4 to 5 dozen cookies

Adapted from "Rumford Everyday Cook Book for the Housekeeper and Student"
Rumford Baking Powder, undated, c. 1900

Brownies

Brownies are a psychological adaptation. They're a piece of chocolate cake in the relatively guilt-free guise of a cookie. They've been an American favorite since the end of the nineteenth century, predating our other national chocolate inspiration, the chocolate chip cookie.

We owe a great deal to Milton Snaveley Hershey, who encountered failure several times before he enjoyed success. In 1876, he borrowed money from his aunt to open a candy shop in Philadelphia. It failed. He opened a small caramel factory. In three years he was bankrupt. He borrowed more money and started over with more caramels, now tissue-wrapped. He almost didn't make it again, but in 1891, he decided to dip his caramels in chocolate. And in 1900, he sold his Lancaster Caramel Company for a million dollars, reserving the right to continue to sell chocolate. He had noticed that children eating his chocolate-covered caramels licked off the coating and threw away the caramels. "Caramels are a fad," he said. "I'll stake everything on chocolate." He was right. He was also right to drop his middle name. Would *you* buy a package of Snaveley's kisses?

½ cup unsalted butter at room temperature plus butter for the baking dish	2 eggs
1 cup flour	½ teaspoon pure vanilla extract
pinch of salt	2 squares (2 ounces) unsweetened chocolate, melted
1 cup sugar	½ cup chopped walnuts

1. Preheat the oven to 350 degrees. Butter an 8-inch square baking dish.
2. Mix the flour with the salt. In a separate bowl, cream the butter. Gradually add the sugar and continue to beat until light and fluffy. Add the eggs one at a time, beating after each. Beat in the vanilla and the chocolate. Gradually add the flour mixture and combine thoroughly. Stir in the walnuts. Spread the batter evenly in the buttered baking dish.
3. Bake for 40 minutes, or until a toothpick poked into the center comes out dry. (A few moist crumbs are fine, but wet batter is not.) Cut into squares and remove from the pan while still warm.

Yield: 12 to 16 brownies

Adapted from "Hershey's Recipes"
Hershey Chocolate Corporation, 1940

Blondies

Blondies are not brownies. That's the beginning of their claim to fame. While Milton Snaveley Hershey may whirl in his grave at the thought of brownies without chocolate, they are excellent nonetheless. Eating them is like discovering a secret or putting aside the obvious and getting to the heart of the matter. The not-a-brownie, better known as a blondie, is a subtle treat, like a wink between friends. I could have been a brownie, they say, but I like myself better this way. In a perfect world, where everybody has a cookie for each hand, one would be a brownie and one would be a blondie.

⅓ cup unsalted butter at room temperature plus butter for the baking dish
⅓ cup sugar
⅓ cup molasses

1 egg
1 cup flour
½ teaspoon baking powder
1 cup chopped pecans or walnuts

1. Preheat the oven to 325 degrees. Butter an 8-inch square baking dish.
2. Cream the butter and gradually add the sugar, continuing to cream, and stopping at least once to scrape down the sides of the mixing bowl. Beat in the molasses and the egg. In a separate bowl, combine the flour with the baking powder and gradually add this mixture to the batter. Beat well, and stir in the nuts. The batter will be thick. Pour or spoon it into the buttered baking dish, levelling the top with a spatula.
3. Bake for 35 minutes, or until golden brown. Cut into squares and remove from the pan while still warm.

Yield: 12 to 16 blondies

Adapted from "Cook Book"
Ceresota Flour, undated

Meringues and Variations

*A*meringue is just a puff of air, a wisp of sugar made crisp, an idea that melts in your mouth. Meringues are next door to magic, a zephyr of a cookie that becomes a memory even before it's gone.

There are wonderful things to be done with meringues. You can scoop out their centers and fill them with whipped cream or ice cream and berries and top them with chocolate sauce or fruit syrup, sandwich two together with jam, or add cocoa to make chocolate kisses, so gentle and sweet, though they hint at wickedness, that they are undoubtedly food for poets as well as for lovers.

And remember, they have no cholesterol. Egg whites and sugar. That's almost all they are.

4 egg whites	1 cup sugar
pinch of salt	1/2 teaspoon pure vanilla extract
1/8 teaspoon cream of tartar	

1. Preheat the oven to 300 degrees. Line a cookie sheet with parchment or waxed paper.
2. Beat the egg whites in a scrupulously clean and dry mixing bowl. As they begin to foam, add the salt and cream of tartar, and continue to beat. As they become firm, slowly and gradually add the sugar and vanilla, beating until the whites are thick and glossy and the sugar is completely dissolved.

3. Using a tablespoon or a pastry bag, form mounds of meringue on the parchment paper, about 2 inches apart. Bake until the meringues are dry and very pale brown. (To make perfectly white meringues, bake at 200 degrees for 3 hours, and let them cool in the turned-off oven.)

Variation: For cocoa meringues, beat 3 egg whites until stiff. Gradually add 1 cup sugar, beating constantly. Add 1 teaspoon pure vanilla extract and $\frac{1}{2}$ teaspoon vinegar and beat for 5 minutes, until stiff and glossy and the sugar is completely dissolved. Stir in $3\frac{1}{2}$ tablespoons cocoa. Drop by tablespoonfuls on a baking sheet covered with parchment or waxed paper. Bake at 275 degrees for 30 minutes, or until dry. You can eat these plain or you can add strawberries, vanilla ice cream, and chocolate whipped cream (see page 88). Yum.

Yield: 2 to 3 dozen meringues

Meringues adapted from ""Home Partners," Certified and Merit Breads, 1924
Cocoa Meringues adapted from "Hershey's Recipes," Hershey Chocolate Corporation, 1940

Orange Lunch Box Cookies

Sometime around 6600 B.C. the wheel was invented. In about 4000 B.C. oranges were cultivated. And the orange crate was hammered together for the first time by inventor E. Bean in 1875. Progress is slow, but inevitable. The crate led to the wide-scale distribution and marketing of oranges, and before too long, oranges were a lunch box staple. With good reason. They are portable, come in their own package (easily unwrapped), and are sweet, juicy, and healthful. A 1916 Sunkist pamphlet tells us that "Oranges . . . ought to be used as freely as the financial ability of the consumer may permit. A laboring man may not be able always to eat oranges at breakfast, yet the fruit is usually very cheap, and the consumption of it will obviate the need of physic and save many a doctor's bill." Put an orange in a cookie!

½ cup unsalted butter plus butter for
  the cookie sheet
1 cup sugar
2 egg yolks
grated rind of 1 orange

¼ cup orange juice
1½ cups flour
2 teaspoons baking powder
¼ teaspoon salt

VICTORY LUNCH BOXES

Never before have wives and mothers been so aware of the importance of making certain that their husbands and children are getting the kind of food which builds and maintains physical fitness and mental alertness. The failure of so many young men to pass the physical examinations for our armed forces, due to the results of faulty nourishment, has done more to stress the value of a well-balanced diet than all the teaching of years gone by.

"Victory Lunch Box Meals"
Pet Evaporated Milk, 1942

THE·SCHOOL LUNCH

EDVCATIONAL·DEPARTMENT
GENERAL·FOODS·CORPORATION
NEW YORK, N.Y.

1. Cream the butter. Gradually add the sugar, continuing to beat until light and fluffy, stopping at least once to scrape down the sides of the bowl. Add the egg yolks and beat thoroughly. Mix in the orange rind and juice. In a separate bowl, combine the flour, baking powder, and salt, and fold this mixture into the batter. Wrap the dough in plastic wrap or aluminum foil and chill for several hours or overnight.

2. Preheat the oven to 375 degrees. Butter a cookie sheet.

3. Remove the dough from the refrigerator, and let it sit at room temperature for a minute or two. Roll the dough out between two sheets of lightly floured waxed paper to a thickness of 1/3 inch. Cut out circles with a biscuit cutter or the floured rim of a glass. Reroll the scraps and cut again. If the dough is too sticky, place it in the freezer for a few minutes. Place the circles at least 2 inches apart on the baking sheet — they spread as they bake.

4. Bake for 15 minutes. For a crisp cookie, bake a minute or two longer. Remove from the pan and cool on a rack. If desired, ice with Orange Frosting. (See page 24 for recipe).

Yield: 2 to 3 dozen cookies, depending on size

Adapted from "Seald Sweet Cook Book"
Florida Citrus Exchange, undated

Chocolate Bittersweet Cookies

The chocolate chip cookie story goes like this: In 1795, Amelia Simmons's *American Cookery* became the first cook book to be published in America. One of its recipes was for a lovely cookie made with both brown and white sugar.

Now it's 1933. Ruth Wakefield is baking cookies for the inn she and her husband own. Her recipe is almost exactly the same as Amelia Simmons's. But she wants to bake *chocolate* cookies, and she's in a rush. She decides that if she adds chopped chocolate pieces to the batter, the chocolate will melt in the oven and she will have saved the time involved in melting it separately. But the chocolate doesn't melt — it stays in separate pieces — and the cookies are wonderful. She names them after her Toll House Inn. Six years later, Nestlé starts distributing chocolate that is *already* chopped. The company buys the rights to the Toll House name and recipe, and packages its chocolate bits in a cellophane bag with a picture of the Toll House Inn in the corner.

And a year after *that*, Hershey publishes its pamphlet of chocolate recipes, including one for chocolate chip cookies that is almost exactly the same as the Nestlé recipe, which is almost exactly the same as the Amelia Simmons recipe, but changes its name to Chocolate Bittersweet Cookies. A cookie by any other name, Shakespeare almost said, still tastes as sweet.

In 1940, when this recipe was published, Hershey's wasn't making bittersweet bits — the recipe includes directions for breaking an eight-ounce bar of Hershey's bittersweet chocolate into little bitty pieces, and a note that if you would rather have milk chocolate cookies, you can simply chop up a large bar of Hershey's milk chocolate to use instead.

1 cup flour	¼ cup granulated (white) sugar
1 teaspoon baking powder	1 egg
⅛ teaspoon salt	½ teaspoon pure vanilla extract
½ cup unsalted butter, at room temperature	⅓ cup walnut pieces
½ cup brown sugar, packed	8 ounces semi-sweet chocolate bits

1. Preheat the oven to 350 degrees.
2. Mix the flour, baking powder, and salt in a small bowl.
3. Cream the butter with the two sugars until it is light and fluffy. Beat in the egg and vanilla.
4. Gradually beat the flour mixture into the butter mixture. Add the nuts and the chocolate and combine thoroughly.
5. Drop by rounded tablespoonfuls onto an ungreased cookie sheet.
6. Bake for 10 minutes, or until golden brown. Let stand on the sheet for 2 to 3 minutes before transferring to wire racks to cool.

Yield: 2 dozen cookies

Adapted from "Hershey's Recipes"
Hershey Chocolate Corporation, 1940

Reprinted from *The Old-Time Brand-Name Cookbook*, by Bunny Crumpacker
Smithmark Publishers, 1998

Chocolate Pinwheels

These are cookies that are fun for children to make, and they're certainly fun for children to eat. The pinwheel effect is pretty, though it verges on fuss for the sake of fuss. I imagine these cookies were popular at old-fashioned tea parties. The thing is that they don't have to be perfect; I think they're even nicer when the pinwheel effect is a little lopsided and splotchy; they look a little more homemade that way. Isn't that a happy thought? Of course, there's nothing wrong with perfection. They're good either way. And a happy reward for patient children.

1½ cups flour
1 teaspoon baking powder
pinch of salt
½ cup unsalted butter at room
  temperature

½ cup sugar
1 egg yolk, lightly beaten
3 tablespoons milk
1 square (1 ounce) unsweetened
  chocolate, melted

The nervousness and peevishness of our times are chiefly attributable to tea and coffee; the digestive organs of confirmed coffee drinkers are in a state of chronic derangement, which reacts upon the brain, producing fretful and lachrymose moods. Cocoa and chocolate are neutral in their physical effects, and are really the most harmless of our fashionable drinks.

Dr. Karl Ernest "Cocoa and Chocolate"
Walter Baker & Company, Ltd., 1917

1. Mix the flour, baking powder, and salt. In a separate bowl, cream the butter and gradually add the sugar. When the mixture is light, add the egg yolk and mix well. Alternately add the flour mixture and milk, and mix until smooth. Divide the batter in half. Add the melted chocolate to one half; and refrigerate the chocolate half while you work with the plain.

2. Place the plain batter on a lightly floured sheet of waxed paper and, using a floured rolling pin, roll it into an ⅛-inch-thick rectangle. Roll up, with the waxed paper, from the narrow edge, and refrigerate while you work with the chocolate batter.

3. Repeat the rolling-out process with the chocolate batter. Leave it in place and unroll the plain batter, placing it over the chocolate sheet and removing the waxed paper. Roll the two layers up together, from the narrow edge, like a jelly roll. Cover with plastic wrap, and refrigerate for at least 12 hours.

4. Preheat the oven to 425 degrees.

5. Unwrap the roll, and cut it into ⅛-inch-thick cookies. Place on an ungreased cookie sheet and bake for 10 minutes. The white part of the cookies may brown slightly; this won't affect the taste, but if you'd rather have the chocolate-vanilla look, lower the heat slightly and watch carefully as the cookies bake.

Yield: 3 dozen cookies

Adapted from "Best Chocolate Recipes"
Walter Baker & Company, Inc., 1932

How to Save Time

When a "job" is done, forget it. Thinking about it is like
   doing it twice.

Keep the ice-box cleared out and clean it daily.

Make enough pie crust at one time for several pies.

Teach the family to pick up their bed rooms while they dress.

What You Can Do with the Time You Save

Attend the Woman's Club, the Woman's Church Society,
   Sewing Club, Parent-Teacher Association, some Lodge,
   the Grange, etc.

   Take up again your music, languages, dancing.

Pies

   Make dainty accessories for yourself or your house.

   Serve informal afternoon tea once or twice a month —
indoors in cold weather — on the piazza or outdoors in
   warm weather.

Do a little gardening.

Read some new books — outdoors in suitable weather.

Visit the shops occasionally.

From "Home Partners" by Ida Bailey Allen
Certified and Merit Breads, 1924

Sour Cream Apple Pie

The power of apples is amply demonstrated by the contretemps in the Garden in Eden and also in the word itself. As the fruit spread throughout northern Europe from its Indo-European roots, the word *abel* went with it: In German, apple is *apfel;* in Dutch, *appel;* in Russian, *jabloko;* in English, *apple.* The Latin word for fruit, *pomum,* became the French *pomme* for apple. The French must have thought apples were an outstanding example of fruit. All these words testify to the enormous gift of apples. From blossom to fruit, they delight the eye and please the palate. We like to think that apple pie is the quintessential American dessert, but in fact, there are ample references to apple pies all the way back to the Middle Ages, long before Columbus set sail. Perhaps that's one reason why apple pie is the perfect American dessert. With its heritage from many cultures and peoples, it is a dessert with ethnic variations. This one (based in part on a recipe from *The New York Times Menu Cookbook*) is rich with sour cream, and ranks with the very best.

1 unbaked 9-inch pie crust
2 eggs, lightly beaten
½ cup sugar plus ⅓ cup
2 tablespoons flour plus 2 additional
   tablespoons
pinch of salt
1 cup sour cream (regular or ⅓ less fat,
   not fat free)

4 tart apples (such as Granny Smiths),
   peeled, cored, and sliced
¼ teaspoon nutmeg, freshly grated
   if possible
3 tablespoons unsalted butter

1. Preheat the oven to 350 degrees. Line a 9-inch pie pan with the unbaked crust.
2. Combine the eggs, ½ cup sugar, 2 tablespoons flour, the salt, and sour cream in a mixing bowl, and add the apples, mixing well. Pour into the pie crust and bake for 10 minutes.
3. While the pie is baking, combine the remaining flour and sugar in a mixing bowl or a food processor bowl. Add the nutmeg and, using a pastry cutter, two knives, or the processor, cut in the butter until the mixture is crumbly. Sprinkle it over the apples and bake for 30 minutes longer, or until the crumbs are brown and the apples are tender.

8 servings

Adapted from "Sour Cream Recipes"
Milk Industry Foundation, undated

START HOUSEKEEPING RIGHT —

WASHBURN-CROSBY CO.
WASHBURN'S
TRADE MARK
Gold
MEDAL
FLOUR
WASHBURN-CROSBY CO.

GOLD MEDAL FLOUR

LET DREAMS COME TRUE

Jam Turnovers

What's special about these flexible treats is their cream cheese crust. It's easy, but it's respectable — you'll still think well of it in the morning. It's remarkably easy to handle. You can prepare it today, and bake it tomorrow; you can freeze it and use it next week; you can use it for a sweet little one-bite baby pie, or for a savory quiche or tart. It doesn't need fussing. It forgives your sins. Of course, it *is* rich. But we're talking pie crust here, not broccoli. You could fill it with broccoli and let the good guys and the bad guys fight it out once they get inside you. Or you could have broccoli for dinner and Jam Turnovers for dessert. That's what I would do.

1 cup unsalted butter (two sticks) at room temperature

8 ounces cream cheese at room temperature (use regular cream cheese, *not* whipped or low fat)

2 cups flour plus flour for rolling out the dough

2 tablespoons sugar

1/4 cup jam or jelly (regular or unsweetened)

1. Cream the butter and cream cheese in a mixing bowl until they are well blended. Add the flour and sugar and mix just until the dough holds together. Form it into a roll about two inches in diameter; cover with plastic wrap and refrigerate for at least 2 hours.
2. Preheat the oven to 400 degrees.
3. Remove the roll from the refrigerator. Turn it out onto a floured surface. Cut crosswise into 1/2-inch-thick slices. Roll out each slice, using a floured rolling pin, to a thickness of about 1/8-inch. Use a biscuit cutter or the floured rim of a glass to cut each slice into a circle. (The size of the circles is up to you — small ones for just a bite; larger ones for more substantial munching.) Reroll the scraps and cut again. Use only as much flour on the surface and the rolling pin as you need; too much will toughen the pastry.

BAG PAPER TEST FOR OVEN TEMPERATURE:

*Place a piece of bag paper on the center
rack of the heated oven.
Count sixty.
If the paper is burnt on the edges,
the oven is "hot" or "quick."
If the paper is lightly and evenly
browned, it is "medium."
If the paper is scarcely colored, it is "cool" or "slow."
This test is helpful in determining the temperature
of the oven, but of course, it is not accurate.*

*"Good Pies"
Nonesuch Mincemeat, undated*

4. Place a dollop of jam — about ½ teaspoon for 2-inch circles — just off center in the mid-dle of each circle. Moisten the tip of your finger with water (fill a cup with water and leave it to one side for finger-dipping) and wet the edge of half of each circle. Fold the other half over onto the moistened edge and press to seal. Use the floured tines of a fork to press around each crescent, making a pattern of indentations and also making the seal tighter. Make a small slit in the center of each turnover or prick each one with a fork.
5. Place the turnovers on a baking sheet. Bake for 15 to 20 minutes, until golden.

Note: To use the crust for a savory filling, omit the sugar. Mushrooms sautéed with minced onion and garlic and a bit of dill or thyme make a lovely savory bite. But for this recipe, remember that much depends on the quality of the jam.

Yield: two dozen 2-inch circle turnovers

Adapted from "Famous Dishes"
Frigidaire, 1936

Blueberry Pie

There isn't much in the way of blue food, but blueberries more than make up for the gap. They are lusciously, deliciously, marvelously, intensely *blue*. And when you eat them, your tongue is blue, your teeth are blue — your mouth, your whole being, is blue. Not sad blue. Happy blue. And blueberry pie is one of the happiest of blues.

4 cups blueberries, fresh or frozen
$\frac{1}{4}$ to $\frac{1}{2}$ cup sugar, depending on the
   sweetness of the berries
pinch of salt
$\frac{1}{4}$ cup water
3 tablespoons quick-cooking tapioca

$\frac{1}{2}$ teaspoon nutmeg, freshly grated
  if possible
unbaked pastry for a 9-inch 2-crust pie
optional glaze: 1 egg, beaten with
  1 tablespoon water; or milk

1. Preheat the oven to 425 degrees.
2. Combine the blueberries and $\frac{1}{4}$ cup sugar (taste to see if more sugar is needed); add the salt, water, tapioca, and nutmeg, and mix.
3. Line a 9-inch pie pan with the bottom crust and fill with the berries. Fit the top crust over the filling; fold the edge under the bottom crust and pinch together to seal, raising the rim all around. Crimp the edges by pinching between your thumb and the knuckle of your second finger, or press the edges with the tines of a fork. Cut a tiny hole in the middle of the crust and make several short slits around the hole. Glaze the top crust by brushing it with the egg and water mixture, or simply by brushing with milk.
4. Bake for 15 minutes; lower the heat to 350 degrees and bake for 20 minutes longer, or until the crust is golden brown.

6 to 8 servings

Adapted from "A Cook's Tour"
Minute Tapioca, 1929

Art Linkletter's Peach Pie

Art Linkletter had a long and varied career on radio and television, and was probably best known for his programs featuring children who said "the darndest things." He began in broadcasting by directing radio shows from the Los Angeles Exposition, the Texas Centennial, and the San Francisco Fair, the pamphlet tells us, and goes on to add that in 1945, he was one of the top six handball players in the country. Playing handball burns off a lot of calories, and his Peach Pie is a lovely way to supply the fuel.

$\frac{3}{4}$ to 1 cup sugar, depending on the sweetness of the peaches

2 tablespoons flour

$\frac{1}{4}$ teaspoon salt

$\frac{1}{2}$ teaspoon nutmeg, freshly grated if possible

8 medium to large peaches, peeled and sliced, or 1 bag (1$\frac{1}{4}$ pounds) frozen peaches

unbaked pastry for a 9-inch 2-crust pie

optional glaze: 1 egg mixed with 1 tablespoon water; or milk

1. Preheat the oven to 425 degrees.
2. Combine $\frac{3}{4}$ cup sugar, the flour, salt, and nutmeg in a mixing bowl. Mix in the peaches, and taste to see if more sugar is needed.
3. Line a 9-inch pie pan with the bottom crust and fill with the peaches. Fit the top crust over the filling; fold the edge under the bottom crust and pinch together to seal, raising the rim all around. Crimp the edges by pinching between your thumb and the knuckle of your second finger, or press the edges with the tines of a fork. Cut a tiny hole in the middle of the crust and cut several short slits around the hole. Glaze the top crust by brushing it with the egg mixture, or simply by brushing with milk.
4. Bake for 5 minutes; then lower the heat to 350 degrees and bake for 35 minutes longer, or until the crust is golden brown.

Note: The pie can be baked without the top crust; for a single-crust pie, bake until the peaches begin to bubble and brown. To peel peaches, dip them into boiling water for 15 seconds; remove them, and immediately plunge them into very cold water.

6 to 8 servings

Adapted from "Cook Book of the Stars"
WFBL, Columbia Broadcasting System Network, 1945

Trauben Kuchen (Grape Pie)

There isn't really a line between cake and pie, there's more of a gulf. But *kuchen* (German for cake) crosses the nonexistent line, and falls into the gulf — or at least this *kuchen* does. It's a pie crust filled with grapes, which means it's really a pie and not a cake in any language. But in the *New York Herald Tribune*'s 1940 publication of "Prize Winning Recipes," this is called a *kuchen*. Of course, the *New York Herald Tribune* doesn't exist any more. How could anyone trust a newspaper that didn't know the difference between a cake and a pie? On the other hand, this is a prize-winning recipe. I suspect that it was someone's old family recipe, and that originally, in Germany, it was made with a *kuchen* batter bottom rather than with a pie crust. It's good this way, and it would be good that way, too.

1 unbaked 9-inch pie crust
¼ cup sugar plus an
    additional ½ cup
3 cups seedless grapes
1 tablespoon cornstarch
1 cup half-and-half
3 eggs, lightly beaten
½ teaspoon cinnamon

1. Preheat the oven to 425 degrees.
2. Line a 9-inch pie pan with the unbaked crust. Sprinkle ¼ cup sugar evenly over the crust. Place the grapes over the sugar.
3. Combine the remaining ½ cup sugar with the cornstarch in a mixing bowl. Gradually add the half-and-half and mix until smooth. Add the eggs and mix thoroughly. Pour this mixture over the grapes, and sprinkle the top with the cinnamon.
4. Bake for 15 minutes; lower the heat to 350 degrees and bake for 30 minutes longer, or until the filling is firm. Serve cold.

6 to 8 servings

Adapted from "Prize Winning Recipes"
New York Herald Tribune, 1940

Jamaican Pumpkin Pie

Ginger was part of the ancient silk trade between China and Europe. Ginger, cinnamon, and silk went one way, and gold and silver, among other things, went the other. It was the first Asian spice to be successfully grown in the Americas— on the island of Jamaica in the Caribbean. Columbus bumped into Jamaica — we like to say he discovered it, but actually, it was there before he arrived in 1494.

Ginger is now a universal spice, used in everything from English gingerbread to Japanese pickled ginger, and with good reason. It not only tastes good, it's good for you as well, aiding digestion and warding off motion sickness. Emphasizing it in pumpkin pie is an inspired idea. Ginger marmalade is on the jam shelf of your supermarket. (If it's not, it should be, so ask.) Try the marmalade on cream cheese or yogurt on an English muffin. And enjoy it in your pumpkin pie.

1½ cups cooked pumpkin
  (fresh or canned), puréed
¼ cup brown sugar, firmly packed
1 teaspoon cinnamon
½ teaspoon salt

2 eggs, lightly beaten
1½ cups milk
½ cup heavy cream
½ cup ginger marmalade
1 unbaked 9-inch pie crust

1. Preheat the oven to 425 degrees.
2. Combine the pumpkin with the brown sugar, cinnamon, salt, and eggs in a mixing bowl. Whisk in the milk and cream, and then the ginger marmalade.
3. Line a 9-inch pie pan with the crust and pour in the pumpkin mixture. Bake for 10 minutes; lower the heat to 325 degrees and bake 40 minutes longer, or until set. A knife inserted into the pie about 1 inch from the edge will come out clean; in the middle, the custard will be almost firm. The pie will continue to cook after it's removed from the oven, so take care not to overbake it. Cool on a rack, and then chill.

Note: It's fine to substitute low-fat or skim milk for the milk and cream. The pie won't be as rich, but it will still have an excellent taste.

6 to 8 servings
Adapted from "Secrets of the Jam Cupboard"
Certo, 1932

Lemon Pie Unique

There's a reason why Sunkist, in its 1939 pamphlet, called this pie "unique." In no way is this your run-of-the-mill lemon meringue pie. Most obviously, there's no meringue. But just as clearly, there's no creamy lemon pudding under the missing meringue. What we have instead are sliced lemons — yes! sliced lemons! — tangy and bright yellow circles of pure lemon, sugary and rich. If you like lemons — *really* like lemons — you'll love this pie. It's *very* lemony. The pie may remind you of lemon bars, or lemon curd, or lemon meringue, but this is the real thing, the lemon McCoy. It's very rich, so serve it in small slices. (You can always have two.) Is it good with vanilla ice cream? Is there a pie in this wonderful world that isn't good with vanilla ice cream?

1 unbaked 8-inch pie crust	2 lemons
1½ cups sugar	1 cup cold water
¾ cup flour	1 tablespoon unsalted butter
1 teaspoon grated lemon zest	

1. Preheat the oven to 425 degrees.
2. Line an 8-inch pie pan with the crust. Grate one of the lemons until you have 1 teaspoon of grated zest. In a mixing bowl, combine the sugar, flour, and lemon zest. Sprinkle 1½ cups of this mixture over the crust.
3. Peel both lemons, removing all the white pith. Cut the lemons into very thin slices, removing the seeds as you go. Place the lemons in the crust, either arranging them in careful circles, or simply piling the lemons in and levelling the top.
4. Sprinkle the remaining sugar mixture over the lemons. Pour the water over the lemons (use less water if it threatens to overflow); stir very gently (without disturbing the lemon slices if you've arranged them in circles) and dot with the butter.
5. Bake for 10 minutes; lower the heat to 325 degrees and bake for 40 to 50 minutes longer, until the lemons are lightly browned. Serve warm.

6 to 8 servings

Adapted from "Sunkist Lemons"
Sunkist, 1939

Two Sweet Potato Pies

*I*feel strongly about sweet potato pie. First of all, we don't eat it often enough. Secondly, we consider it an example of Southern cooking (which it is) rather than a national treasure (which it also is). Thirdly, we usually smother it in too many spices, just as we do pumpkin pie, so that the special taste of the sweet potato is lost in a mist of cinnamon and nutmeg and cloves.

Sweet potato pie is a beautiful color, it's full of vitamin A, and it's naturally sweet. This is a sweet potato pie with an unusual variation. Just don't use canned sweet potatoes. Don't even think about it.

2 cups boiled sweet potatoes, (about 3
   large) mashed
2 cups milk
3 eggs, lightly beaten
1½ cups sugar

¼ teaspoon salt
1 teaspoon pure lemon or vanilla extract
pinch of nutmeg, freshly grated if
   possible
1 unbaked 9-inch pie crust

1. Preheat the oven to 375 degrees.
2. Combine the sweet potatoes with the milk, eggs, sugar, salt, lemon or vanilla extract, and nutmeg in a mixing bowl. Mix well.
3. Line a 9-inch pie pan with the unbaked crust, and pour in the sweet potato filling.
4. Bake for 40 to 50 minutes, until a clean, dry knife inserted an inch from the edge comes out clean. Don't overbake: The middle won't be set, but it will continue to cook after the pie is removed from the oven.

6 to 8 servings

Adapted from "Royal Cook Book"
Standard Brands Inc., 1930

Variation: In 1910, Gold Medal Flour published a pamphlet which included this recipe for "A Different Sweet Potato Pie:" Boil 3 large sweet potatoes for 20 minutes; cool, peel, and cut into thick slices. Line a deep-dish pie pan with an unbaked crust. Arrange the sliced potatoes in layers, sprinkling each layer with sugar, cinnamon, and nutmeg (in all, use about ½ cup sugar and ½ teaspoon each of cinnamon and nutmeg). Pour 3 tablespoons whiskey, rum, or Cognac over the sweet potatoes, and follow with ½ cup water. Bake as is, or cover with a top crust, cutting a few slits in the top for steam to escape. Bake at 350 degrees for 40 minutes, or until the top crust is golden. Serve warm.

CREAM — CREAM — CREAM! You can't serve your family or guests too much . . . . for everyone loves our delicious, fresh, thick cream on fruits, cereals, soups, salads, desserts! Keep a sufficient supply in the refrigerator. Order now!

"The Sealtest Food Adviser"
Sheffield Farms, 1939

Puddings and Frozen Desserts

There seems to be a rather general feeling that desserts frozen in the electric refrigerator are expensive luxuries. As a matter of fact, the careful analysis of a collection of tested recipes shows that on the whole the cost of desserts frozen at home in the electric refrigerator is unexpectedly low.

"Cooking with Cold"
Kelvinator, 1933

Bread Pudding

Bread pudding is a model of what a pudding ought to be, sweet and soft, solid and sturdy, not insubstantial but not heavy either. It is a poetic and philosophic dish that nourishes and delights. Of all the puddings, bread pudding is perhaps the most practical and the most ethereal. It is practical because it uses what's left of the daily loaf, and ethereal because it turns that hearty loaf into a custardy sweetness, reminiscent of the dairy as well as the hearth. There are bread puddings with raspberries embedded in their middles like rubies. There are bread puddings served with elaborate sauces and designs. And there are bread puddings that are no more than bread, eggs, milk, and sugar, with perhaps a bit of vanilla. They are all works of wonder. Bread pudding is the sweet staff of life.

2 tablespoons melted unsalted butter plus
  butter for the baking dish
2 to 3 cups dry bread, cubed (see note)
2 cups milk
¼ cup sugar

2 eggs, lightly beaten
½ teaspoon pure vanilla extract
¼ teaspoon salt
½ teaspoon *each* cinnamon and nutmeg
  or 1 tablespoon brown sugar

1. Preheat the oven to 350 degrees. Butter an 8-inch square baking dish.
2. Arrange the bread cubes evenly in the baking dish. Add the milk, butter, sugar, eggs, vanilla, and salt. Stir gently until all the bread is moistened. Let stand for 10 minutes and stir again. If you are using the spices, add them now and stir them in gently.
3. Bake for 45 minutes to 1 hour, until the top is browned. If you are using the brown sugar, sprinkle it evenly over the top of the pudding and set it under the broiler until it bubbles and melts. Watch carefully to prevent burning.

Note: Use the best possible bread — a homemade or bakery loaf, or substantial packaged bread like Pepperidge Farm or Arnold. Everything depends on the quality of your ingredients.

6 servings

Adapted from "Be an Artist at the Gas Range"
The Mystery Chef and Your Gas Company, 1935

Marshmallow Delight

What is a marshmallow? A playful puff, a wisp, a softness of sugar and air, a charred but sweet nibble on a stick after the scary story around the campfire. But once, marshmallows were more serious. They were made with the gummy extract of the root of the mallow plant, a perennial that grows in swamps and marshes. Yuk. Packaged and formed with gelatin instead of mallow root, they were all the rage in the 1920s and '30s. Marshmallow Fluff came along (remember Fluffer-Nutter sandwiches?) in the early 1920s, developed by a fellow with the felicitous name of Archibald Query. After some years of peddling his goo door-to-door, Mr. Query sold his sticky formula for $500 to the Durkee-Mower Company, which owns it still.

1 20-ounce can crushed pineapple,
    canned in its own juice, drained
2 cups marshmallows (either large
    and quartered, or small)
1 cup heavy cream

1. Combine the drained pineapple and the marshmallows in a mixing bowl and refrigerate for several hours. Just before serving, whip the cream and fold it in.

Note: If the pudding is too sweet, add a few drops of lemon juice. The pamphlet suggests serving with sponge cake. Why not? But it's good plain.

6 servings

Adapted from
"Hawaiian Pineapple
as 100 Good Cooks
Serve It"
Dole Pineapple, 1927

Pasha op Paska (A Russian Easter Dish)

ashka means Easter in Russian, and Pashka, or Pasha as this pamphlet calls it, is the traditional Russian Easter dessert. It is a kind of cheesecake, unbaked and made sublime with butter, sour cream, and cream or cottage cheese. In Russia, the dessert is poured into a pyramid-shaped mold with holes for drainage. When it's ready, it's decorated with almonds and candied fruits and taken to the church to be blessed by the priest. It is traditionally eaten with sweet bread, and it's wonderful that way (try panettone, brioche, or challah). It is also marvelous with fresh berries, a sweet berry sauce, or sliced peaches. When you get right down to it, it's divine spread on toasted pound cake — or just plain toast. Or go straight to heaven and just eat it with a spoon.

12 ounces cream cheese at room temperature
½ cup unsalted butter at room temperature
½ cup sour cream

½ cup sugar
Optional: any or all — ¾ cup candied orange peel, ⅓ cup dried currants, 1 cup sliced or chopped almonds

1. Mix all the ingredients together. Line a colander with two layers of rinsed and squeezed out cheesecloth, and fill with the cheese mixture. Cover with more rinsed and squeezed cheesecloth. Place a small dish over the top and a weight on top of the dish, a large can of tomatoes, for instance, or some heavy stones. Place the colander over a bowl to drain. Place in the refrigerator for at least 12 hours. Unmold, removing the cheesecloth. Serve plain, or with sweet or sour cream, or fresh or cooked fruit.

8 to 12 servings

Adapted from "Around the World Cook Book"
Kalamazoo Stoves, 1950

Three Rice Puddings

ecause you can't have too much of a good thing, here are three recipes, count 'em, three, for rice pudding.

A thought about origins and etymologies: rice came west from Asia, where it was first cultivated about 5,500 years ago. A lot of rice words sound the same: in Greek *oruza*, Latin *oryza*, Russian *ris*, German *reis*, Dutch *rijst*, Danish and Swedish *ris*, Italian *riso*, Spanish *aroz*, French *riz*, and English *rice*, probably all from the Sanskrit *vrihi*, or the Afghan *vrize*. Like those words, the puddings made from rice go around the world like a theme with variations. Once, rice was expensive and rare outside Asia. It was treated like a spice rather than a basic food. But when it advanced onto the menu, it was first in the form of rice pudding. These three recipes, beginning with the most traditional, are delectable reasons for putting pudding first.

Creamy Rice Pudding

½ cup sugar	½ cup rice
½ teaspoon salt	butter for the baking dish
5 cups milk	1 teaspoon pure vanilla extract

1. Mix the sugar, salt, and 4 cups of the milk in the top of a double boiler. Heat over hot water in the lower pan and bring to the scalding point, when small bubbles form around the edge of the pan. Gradually add the rice, stirring constantly. Cover and simmer slowly until the rice is tender, about 2 hours.

2. Heat the oven to 375 degrees and butter an 8-inch square baking dish. Add the remaining cup of milk and the vanilla to the rice, stir well, and transfer to the buttered dish. Bake for 20 to 30 minutes, or until a light brown crust has formed.

6 servings

Adapted from "Be an Artist at the Gas Range"
The Mystery Chef and Your Gas Company, 1935

Chocolate Rice Pudding

1 cup milk

1 cup cooked rice

4 tablespoons cocoa

½ cup sugar

pinch of salt

½ teaspoon pure vanilla extract

cream for serving

1. Mix the milk, rice, cocoa, sugar, and salt in the top of a double boiler. Heat over hot water in the lower pan and cook until thick. Cool slightly, add the vanilla and stir. Serve with cream.

4 to 6 servings

Adapted from "Rice — 200 Delightful Ways to Serve It"
Southern Rice Industry, 1935

Hawaiian Cream Pudding

½ cup rice

2 cups milk

¼ cup sugar

pinch of salt

1 cup crushed pineapple, canned in its own juice, well drained

1 teaspoon pure vanilla extract

1 cup heavy cream

1. Mix the rice, milk, sugar, and salt in the top of a double boiler. Heat over hot water in the lower pan. Cook until the rice is tender, 1½ to 2 hours. Cool. Add the pineapple and vanilla and stir. Whip the cream, and fold it into the rice mixture. Chill.

4 to 6 servings

Adapted from "The Everyday Cook Book for the Housekeeper and Student" Rumford Baking Powder, undated

Clean-Up Week: Won't you please search your cellar for empty milk bottles and return them? We will appreciate your cooperation.

"A Year of Recipes"
Abbott's Dairies, 1933

Chocolate Bavarian Cream

Bavaria is in southern Germany, but doesn't seem to have much to do with Bavarian cream, a light and fluffy creation whose roots are French — it was originally a crème bavaroise. Bavarian creams are usually made with gelatin in a custard base, lightened with beaten egg whites and whipped cream, and flavored with fruit or vanilla. This one is much simpler, but does not suffer at all for its innocence. Its heart and soul are chocolate and whipped cream. Not bad for the anatomy of a dessert!

1 tablespoon unflavored gelatin	⅓ cup sugar
¼ cup cold water	2 cups heavy cream
½ cup milk	1 teaspoon pure vanilla
2 squares (2 ounces)	extract
unsweetened chocolate	pinch of salt

1. Sprinkle the gelatin over the cold water in a small cup. Allow to stand for 5 minutes, or until the grains are softened and swollen.
2. In a small saucepan, add the chocolate to the milk and place over low heat. Stir occasionally, until the chocolate has melted. Add the gelatin and whisk until it is completely dissolved. Add the sugar, continuing to stir until it too has dissolved.
3. Set the saucepan over a bowl of cold water and let it sit, stirring occasionally, until it begins to thicken.
4. Meanwhile, whip the cream until stiff. Add the vanilla and salt. Fold the chocolate mixture into the whipped cream.
5. Moisten a mold or serving bowl by running it under cold water. Turn it over so the excess water drips out, but let it stay wet. Pour the chocolate cream into the wet mold. Refrigerate for 3 to 4 hours, or until the cream is firm.

Note: The pudding is also good soft, after only a brief chilling period; it's just different, more like a sauce than a pudding. For a frozen dessert on a hot day, put the bowl in the freezer instead of the refrigerator. Let it soften in the refrigerator for 10 minutes or so before serving.

6 servings

Adapted from "Desserts, Salads, Candies, and Frozen Dishes"
Knox Gelatin, 1933

Lemon Ice

What is the difference between ices and sherbets and sorbets and ice cream? You could say it is a matter of complications. Ices are just fruit, sugar, and water. Ice cream gets more involved, with a cream or custard base. Sherbet is in the middle. Sorbet is just the French word for sherbet.

The making of iced desserts goes way back. Marco Polo wrote of ice in China that was brought down from the mountains and scraped and flavored with fruits. Aztecs may have poured chocolate into snow, just as some old New England cookbooks have recipes for newly fallen snow mixed with cream and vanilla extract. In a world where some brave soul tasted oysters for the first time and somebody else discovered cheese, mixing snow or scraped ice with fruit flavoring must have required much less courage, and probably happened in many places with many variations.

In our day and age, ices are the perfect low-fat dessert. (Unless you serve cookies with them.) And lemon ice, a perennial favorite, is best of all.

3 cups water
1 cup sugar
½ cup freshly squeezed lemon juice

1. Place the water and sugar in a medium saucepan without stirring; bring to a boil, lower the heat, and simmer for 5 minutes.
2. Stir in the lemon juice. Cool. Strain into a bowl and place in the freezer.
3. When the mixture begins to freeze around the edges, mix it well with a fork or a whisk to prevent crystals from forming. Continue to freeze for several hours or until firm.
4. Before serving, let stand for about 10 minutes at room temperature in order to soften slightly.

Note: To make Orange Ice, use orange juice instead of lemon. A bit of grated zest can be added to either of the ices.

6 to 8 servings

Adapted from "Sunkist Recipes"
California Fruit Growers Exchange, 1916

Russian Coffee Frappé

*I*t's 1907, and Teddy Roosevelt is having a cup of coffee at a hotel in Nashville, Tennessee. The coffee he's drinking is a blend developed in the 1880s by a local resident. "Ah!" says Teddy, as he drains his cup, "Good to the last drop!" The hotel is the Maxwell House, and it is famous for its coffee. (For the record, Caleb Chase and James Sanborn — anybody remember Chase and Sanborn? — were the first to put ground coffee in sealed tin cans, in 1878.)

According to some, Russian coffee is half coffee and half cocoa. We call this mocha, and it is delicious. So is this frozen version of coffee, cocoa, and whipped cream. It's creamy and good and surprisingly refreshing.

2 cups hot, freshly brewed coffee	1 cup heavy cream
1 cup sugar	1 teaspoon pure vanilla extract
2 cups freshly made cocoa (see note)	cinnamon
pinch of salt	

1. Pour the hot coffee over the sugar in a heatproof bowl or saucepan and stir until the sugar is dissolved. Add the cocoa and the salt and stir. Cool.
2. Whip the cream until it's thick, and stir in the vanilla. Fold the cream into the coffee mixture until thoroughly blended. Pour into a mold or serving bowl and place in the freezer for 3 hours, or until frozen. Dust the top lightly with cinnamon. Soften in the refrigerator for 10 to 15 minutes before serving.

Note: To make the cocoa, mix 2 heaping teaspoons cocoa and 4 teaspoons sugar in a heatproof cup (a large Pyrex measuring cup works well) or a small saucepan. Stir in a teaspoon or two of milk or cream to make a thick paste and then add hot milk, cream, or water (or a mixture) to make 2 cups.

8 servings

Adapted from "Coffee or Tea?"
Maxwell House Coffee, undated, c. 1925

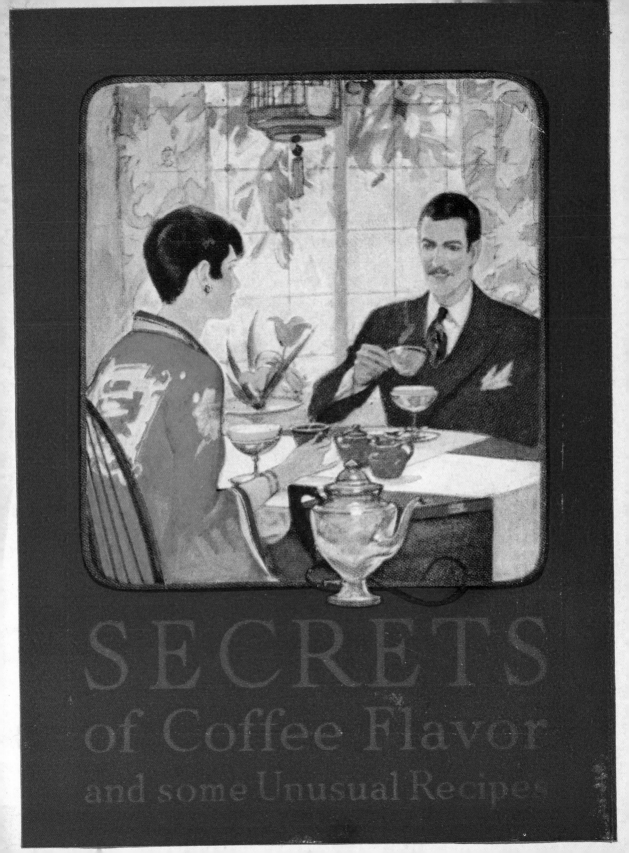

SECRETS

of Coffee Flavor

and some Unusual Recipes

Vienna Coffee

This sweetly simple recipe is adapted from a pamphlet published in 1894 by the manufacturer of the Jewett Table Kettle, "to show the great variety of 'elegant and palatable' beverages which can be made by the use of boiling water." Inevitably, most of the recipes are variations of coffee, cocoa, and tea, but the pamphlet also includes some very odd drinks. For instance, Emergency Punch is made with green tea, brandy, rum, Champagne, and Chartreuse, all mixed together and sweetened with a syrup made from oranges, lemons, sugar, water, cloves, and mace. Boiling water is then added "as desired." But this beverage is an emergency in itself! Recommended for those not feeling well (after the crisis or otherwise), Toast Water is made from stale white bread that has been toasted, steeped in boiling water, and strained. The resulting liquid is served with sugar and cream.

An antidote to Toast Water is this Vienna Coffee, with added ice cream. In 1894, ice cream was still a luxury, but in the spirit of Vienna, it surely should be part of this wonderful coffee, hot or cold.

FOR EACH SERVING
¾ cup chilled coffee
1 scoop vanilla ice cream

3 tablespoons whipped cream
cinnamon

1. Pour chilled coffee into a glass; add ice cream, top with whipped cream, and add a dusting of cinnamon. Serve immediately.

Note: For hot Vienna Coffee, pour hot coffee into a cup or mug; add ice cream, whipped cream, and cinnamon.

One serving

Adapted from "Five O'Clock Tea"
The John C. Jewett Manufacturing Company, 1894

Cranberry Sherbert

Marshwort was once another name for cranberry. Can you imagine eating turkey with marshwort sauce? It is a shame to limit marshworts — or cranberries — to Thanksgiving and Christmas. They can do so much more than accompany a turkey or decorate a tree. Even though they are not available in stores all year, they are easy to freeze. Just take the package out of your grocery bag and put it in the freezer. That's all. Frozen cranberries keep for months, and their sauce is as good in May as it is in November. Fresh or frozen, there are dozens of other lovely things that can be done with cranberries, one of which is cranberry sherbet.

4 cups cranberries
2½ cups cold water plus ½ cup for
   softening the gelatin
2 cups sugar

1 teaspoon unflavored gelatin (⅓ of an
   individual package)
juice of 2 lemons, strained

1. Cook the cranberries and 2½ cups of water in a large saucepan until the berries stop popping, about 10 minutes. Strain, pushing hard with the back of a spoon against the solids in the strainer. Pour the juice back into the saucepan and add the sugar. Cook, stirring, until the sugar is completely dissolved.

2. Sprinkle the gelatin over ½ cup of cold water in a small cup and let sit for 5 minutes, or until the grains are softened and swollen. Add to the hot cranberry juice and stir until completely dissolved. Add the lemon juice.

3. Pour into a freezing pan (a bowl, mold, or pan) and place in the freezer for at least 2 to 3 hours, stirring with a fork or whisk every half hour or so to prevent crystals from forming.

8 servings

Adapted from "Fascinating Cranberries"
Eatmor Cranberries, American Cranberry Exchange,
undated

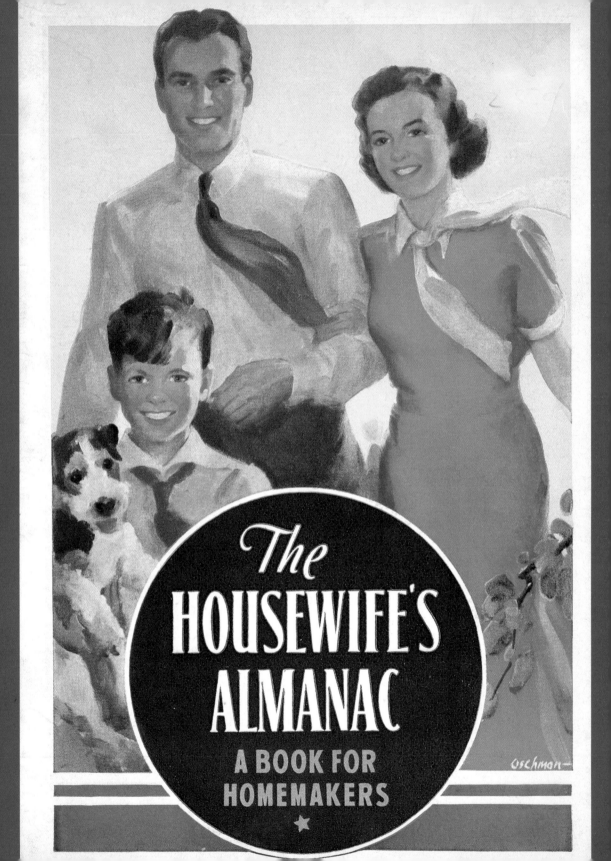

The
HOUSEWIFE'S
ALMANAC
A BOOK FOR HOMEMAKERS
★

*F*ine flavor in fruits is what "good breeding" is in people. One is just as much a matter of careful cultivation as the other. Both are developed only under the most favorable environment.

"Tempting Davis Recipes"
Davis Baking Powder, 1925

Fruit Desserts

Apple Custard

pple Custard is not to be confused with custard apple. The latter is a tropical fruit that can be eaten with a spoon and is supposed to taste like custard. Apple Custard tastes exactly like custard because it *is* custard, poured over gently cooked apples and their juice. You can further the gilding process if you like by topping all, according to the pamphlet, with a meringue. I opt for the relative simplicity of cooked sugared apples and custard. It has a very nurturing taste. This is comfort food, pure and not-so-simple.

6 apples (Granny Smith or Golden
Delicious)
1 cup sugar plus an additional ¼ cup
1 cup cold water
juice of 1 lemon (about 4 tablespoons)
2 cups milk

1 teaspoon cornstarch
3 egg yolks or 2 whole eggs
pinch of salt
1 teaspoon pure vanilla extract

1. Peel, core, and quarter the apples. Place in a saucepan and add 1 cup of the sugar, water, and lemon juice. Cook, covered, over low heat until the apples are tender but still hold their shape, about 15 minutes. Using a slotted spoon, remove the apple pieces and place them in the bottom of a serving dish.

2. Continue cooking the juice left in the saucepan, over medium-high heat, until it is thick and syrupy, about 15 minutes. Pour over the apples.

3. Mix 1 teaspoon of the milk with the cornstarch to form a thick paste. Heat the remaining milk in a saucepan to the scalding point, when small bubbles form around the edges of the pan. In the meantime, beat the eggs, the remaining $1/4$ cup sugar, and the salt with a whisk until blended. Slowly add the hot milk to the egg mixture, and return to the saucepan. Stir in the cornstarch. Cook over low heat, stirring constantly with a wooden spoon, until the mixture thickens. (175 degrees on a candy thermometer; without a candy thermometer, when steam begins to rise from the pan remove the spoon and run your fingertip down the back of its bowl. If your finger leaves a clear path, the custard is done. What's important is to work quickly, so the eggs don't scramble.) Remove from the heat, cool slightly, and add the vanilla. Pour the cooled custard over the apples. Refrigerate until ready to serve.

6 servings

Adapted from "Davis Cook Book"
Davis Baking Powder, undated, c. 1905

Brown Betty

Brown betties, fools, buckles, grunts, slumps, cobble . . . What strange names some fruit desserts have! What are they? A cobbler is a biscuit-type batter spread over fruit and baked. Slumps are similar, but made with a looser batter — you could say it slumps on the plate. Grunts are another variation, in which the dough steams on the top of the fruit, like a dumpling in a stew — some say it makes grunting sounds as it simmers. Buckles are made with cake batter on the bottom of the pan and fruit on top; while they bake, some of the batter buckles and bubbles up. Fools are not a bit foolish, but they *are* simple: just whipped cream swirled into sweetened and puréed fruit. Brown betties are fruit, usually apples, layered with buttered bread crumbs and baked. I don't know who Betty was, but she was one smart cook.

5 slices firm white bread (like Pepperidge
   Farm or Arnold)
4 tablespoons unsalted butter plus butter
   for the baking dish
6 apples

1 teaspoon lemon juice
$^3/_4$ cup sugar
$^1/_2$ teaspoon cinnamon
$^1/_2$ teaspoon nutmeg, freshly
   grated if possible

1. Preheat the oven to 325 degrees. Butter an 8-inch square baking dish.
2. Blend the bread and butter in a food processor to make buttered bread crumbs. If you don't have a processor, melt the butter in a frying pan and stir in the finely crumbled bread. Place a layer of the crumbs in the baking dish.
3. Peel, core, and quarter the apples, and slice each quarter into quarters. Sprinkle the apples with the lemon juice, and mix to coat. In a separate bowl, combine the sugar, cinnamon, and nutmeg. Place a layer of apples over the bread crumbs and sprinkle with some of the sugar mixture. Add another layer of crumbs, and continue to make alternating layers of apples, sugar, and crumbs, ending with bread crumbs.
4. Bake for 45 minutes, or until the top is browned and the apples are soft. Serve with whipped cream or vanilla ice cream.

6 servings

Adapted from "Good Things to Eat"
Fleischmann Company, 1912

Baked Bananas

Ce take bananas for granted. Everybody knows what to do with them; you just peel and eat. Once, they were exotic treats, and we had to learn what to do with them. The pamphlet this recipe comes from has a drawing of the ripening stages of bananas. "Yellow ripe bananas," it says, "can be readily digested by any healthy person." And bananas were so luxurious then that all the recipes were created by the former chef to King Albert of Belgium.

We also take bananas for granted by limiting their potential in the kitchen. We eat them raw and we make banana cream pie and banana bread. And then we stop. But there are a zillion things to do with bananas. (Banana Marmalade! Meat Loaf with Bananas! says the King's chef.) Baked Bananas are just the beginning, but they're a fine way to start.

1 tablespoon unsalted butter	6 teaspoons brown sugar
6 bananas	6 tablespoons water

1. Preheat the oven to 350 degrees. Use about a teaspoon of the butter to grease an 8-inch square baking dish.
2. Peel the bananas and slice them in half, lengthwise. Place them in the baking dish. Sprinkle with the sugar and pour the water around them. Dot with the remaining butter.
3. Bake until the bananas are translucent and the sauce is syrupy. Serve with cream, whipped cream, or vanilla ice cream.

Note: Try using orange or apple juice, white wine, or rum instead of water.

6 servings

Adapted from "From the Tropics to Your Table"
Fruit Dispatch Company, 1926

Milton Berle's Peach Cobbler

*I*n 1945, when the "The Cook Book of the Stars" was published, Milton Berle was the side-splitting star of Eversharp's glittering radio show, 'Let Yourself Go!' Before that, he was a vaudeville star, and after that, a television star — everybody's much loved Uncle Miltie, a three-media favorite. If it's hard to think of him cooking up a storm, just imagine a little frilly apron, a semi-circle edged in ruffles, tied around his waist, over his suit jacket. This unusual Peach Cobbler was his contribution to the "Cook Book of the Stars."

2 tablespoons unsalted butter, plus butter for the baking dish
2 15-ounce cans peaches, canned in juice
1 teaspoon cinnamon
½ teaspoon nutmeg
1 8-ounce box corn muffin mix

2 tablespoons sugar
6 tablespoons water
FOR THE SAUCE:
1 cup of juice reserved from the peaches
1 tablespoon cornstarch
1 teaspoon unsalted butter

1. Preheat the oven to 350 degrees. Butter an 8-inch square baking dish.
2. Drain the peaches, reserving the juice. Mix the peaches with the cinnamon and nutmeg and place in the baking dish.
3. Combine the muffin mix with the sugar; cut in the butter, using two knives, a pastry blender, or a food processor. Add the water and stir. The batter will be very thick.

4. Spoon the batter over the peaches, spreading it as evenly as possible — it doesn't have to reach the sides. Bake for 20 minutes, or until the top is well browned.
5. Mix 1 tablespoon of the reserved peach juice with the cornstarch to form a smooth paste. Heat the remaining juice in a saucepan over medium heat, and when it's hot, gradually whisk in the cornstarch mixture. Stir until the sauce thickens. Remove from the heat and stir in the butter.
6. Serve the sauce hot with the warm cobbler. If you want to add a dollop of whipped cream or a scoop of vanilla ice cream, who would stop you?

6 servings

Adapted from "The Cook Book of the Stars"
WFBL, 1945

Roast Peaches

We have grown used to roasted vegetables, with their marvelous colors and deeply intense flavors. But we don't often roast fruits, which is a shame, because the same thing happens to roasted fruits as to vegetables. Flavor intensifies. Roast peaches (or nectarines, pears, or plums) are an excellent example of the process.

unsalted butter for the baking dish
peaches
FOR EACH PEACH:
½ teaspoon white or brown sugar

¼ teaspoon unsalted butter
lemon juice
nutmeg, freshly grated if possible
water or juice (see note)

1. Preheat the oven to 350 degrees. Butter a baking dish large enough to hold the number of peaches you are using.
2. Peel the peaches by dipping them into boiling water for 10 seconds; remove them, and immediately plunge them into very cold water. The skins should slip off easily. Halve the peaches and remove the pits.
3. Place the peaches, pitted side up, in the baking dish. Fill each cavity with a mixture of the sugar, butter, a few drops of lemon juice, and a sprinkle of nutmeg. Add water or juice to the baking dish to a depth of about ½ inch.
4. Bake for 30 to 45 minutes, until the peaches are lightly browned. Serve hot with plain or whipped cream, or vanilla ice cream.

Note: Use apple, peach, or pear juice, or any other juice (or wine) you prefer.

Adapted from "Kerr Home
Canning Book"
Kerr Glass Mfg. Corp., 1943

Compote des Poires (Compote of Pears)

A compote is a dessert of fruit gently cooked in a sugar syrup and flavored with cinnamon or vanilla. We don't often get excited about compotes, perhaps because we tend to think of them as a winter dessert, a make-do of dried fruit cooked in syrup, a wintry reminder of summer's bounty. But compotes made with fresh fruit are simple to prepare, elegant to behold, and refreshing to eat — worth getting excited about. There are good reasons why compotes are classic French desserts. This compote is made with pears, but similar steps could be used for peaches, plums, nectarines, berries — almost any fruit, and it would still be called a compote or simply poached fruit. And it would still be lovely

6 pears
cold water
freshly squeezed lemon
   juice
2 cups sugar
1 stick cinnamon

DELECTABLE FRUIT COMPOTE

1. Peel the pears, leaving them whole but keeping their stems attached. As you peel each pear, drop it into a bowl of cold water mixed with a few drops of lemon juice.

2. Combine the sugar and 1 cup fresh, cold water in a large saucepan and bring to a boil. Lower the heat and simmer for 8 minutes. Add the cinnamon stick. Drain the pears and add them to the hot syrup. Cover and cook gently for 15 to 20 minutes, until the pears are tender but not mushy. Remove them from the syrup and place them, with their stems upright, in a large bowl.

3. Continue to cook the poaching liquid until it thickens and becomes syrupy. Cool slightly, and then pour over the pears. Serve at room temperature or chilled.

6 servings

Adapted from "Around the World Cook Book"
Kalamazoo Stove and Furnace Company, 1951

Pear Trifle

A trifle is an inconsequential thing, something that doesn't matter very much. But when it's a dessert, a trifle is much greater than the sum of its small parts: cake, custard, fruit, jam, and sherry, all slathered with whipped cream and carefully layered in a big glass bowl. A 1755 recipe includes biscuits, ratafias, macaroons, sack, and custard, all covered with syllabub. It's described as "fit to go to the King's table." This is a simple, more democratic trifle, and while it may be a tiny bit — just a trifle — unorthodox, it is still, in its way, elaborate. No sensible king would pass it up.

2 cups milk

3 egg yolks or 2 whole eggs

¼ cup sugar

pinch of salt

1 teaspoon pure vanilla extract

12 slices pound cake (fresh or frozen)

6 pears, peeled, cored, halved, and lightly
poached, or canned in their own juice

1 cup heavy cream, whipped

optional garnish: unsalted shelled
pistachio nuts or candied fruit

1. Make a custard sauce by heating the milk in a medium-sized saucepan to the scalding point, when small bubbles form around the edge of the pan. Meanwhile, in a separate bowl, whisk the eggs, sugar, and salt together until thoroughly blended. Gradually pour the hot milk into the egg mixture, whisking constantly. Then pour the mixture back into the saucepan. Cook over low heat, stirring constantly with a wooden spoon, until the mixture thickens. (175 degrees on a candy thermometer; without a candy thermometer, when steam begins to rise from the pan remove the spoon and run your fingertip down the back of its bowl. If your finger leaves a clear path, the custard is done. What's important is to work quickly, so the eggs don't scramble.) Immediately remove from the heat and allow to cool. Stir in the vanilla.

2. Place the slices of pound cake on a serving plate, and top each slice with a pear half. (Cut a thin slice off the rounded side of the pear halves so they'll stay flat.) Pour the custard sauce over the pears and cake. Decorate with the whipped cream, and, if you like, scatter the nuts or fruits (or both!) on top.

6 to 12 servings

Adapted from "The Del Monte Fruit Book"
California Packing Corporation, 1926

Shortcakes, Strawberry and Otherwise

S trawberry shortcake is as American as apple pie, even though both apple pie and shortcake were originally English. No matter. Shortcake is now an American classic. It frequently gets confused with short*bread*, which is a buttery cookie, and with just plain cake. Shortcake is short — not in height, silly, but in crispness — because it's made with butter (or lard or vegetable shortening, depending on your heritage). In fact, a shortcake is a biscuit, sweetened because it's being used as a dessert. It is delicious, delightful, and delovely made with strawberries, but it's just as good and more surprising made with sliced peaches, pitted cherries, blueberries, raspberries, sliced plums, nectarines . . . Happy thoughts, all.

I feel sure no one would ever serve a makeshift shortcake with sponge cake if they knew how easy it is to make the real thing with perfect biscuits.

"Be an Artist at the Gas Range"
The Mystery Chef and Your Gas
Company, 1935

5 tablespoons unsalted butter, plus butter
   for the baking pan
2 cups flour
4 teaspoons baking powder
½ teaspoon salt
2 tablespoons sugar

¾ to 1 cup milk
fruit and sugar (1 quart strawberries,
   for example, and ½ cup brown
   or white sugar)
1 cup heavy cream, whipped

1. Preheat the oven to 400 degrees. Butter an 8-inch cake pan or a cookie sheet.

2. Combine the flour, baking powder, salt, and sugar in a food processor or mixing bowl. Either cut in the butter, using a pastry blender, two knives, or your fingers, or pulse briefly to combine. Add the milk, as much as needed (usually, depending on the humidity, among other things, just under a cup) to make a dough that barely holds together. Either turn into the cake pan and pat into

shape, or roll out on a lightly floured board and use a biscuit cutter or the floured rim of a glass to make 2-inch biscuits. (Try to work quickly with the dough and to use a minimum of flour while rolling it out, to keep the biscuits tender.) Place the biscuits on the cookie sheet.

3. Bake for 15 to 20 minutes, until golden brown.
4. Remove from the oven, and split in half horizontally. (Some people like to butter their shortcakes. This is entirely up to you.)
5. While the shortcakes are baking, prepare the fruit. Slice a quart of strawberries, leaving 12 whole. Add the sugar (tasting to see if more is needed) to the berries and let stand until juice forms. At serving time (the shortcakes should be warm — reheat in the oven briefly if you have to), spoon dollops of strawberries and juice on the bottom layers of the shortcakes, cover with the tops, and add more strawberries over all. Top with whipped cream, and, for each serving, 2 whole strawberries.

Note: Prepare other fruits in the same way. Peel and pit peaches, nectarines, or plums, slice thinly, mix with sugar, and let stand to make juice. Raspberries can be mixed with sugar just as the strawberries are, but without slicing. Blueberries are wonderful if some of them are stewed briefly with a bit of sugar (add a little cinnamon or freshly grated nutmeg if you like); then combine the cooked and cooled blueberries with fresh whole berries to serve. Another way of serving shortcake is to present the parts — biscuits, fruit, and whipped cream — in separate bowls and let your guests help themselves.

6 servings

Adapted from "Be an Artist at the Gas Range"
The Mystery Chef and Your Gas Company, 1935

*I*f you were to ask me how to give a "professional touch" to your every-day desserts, I should tell you not to bother preparing *elaborate dishes* at all, but to go straight along with your gelatines and tapiocas,

fruits, berries, puddings and pastries; *looking to your sauces!* Chances are, your desserts, excellent in themselves, are eloquently

Frostings and Sauces

incomplete for want of an appropriate sauce to "dress them up!"

And there is the whole secret of the *fine art* of dessert making!

"Hip-O-Lite Recipes"
Marshmallow Cream, undated

Cream Cheese Date-Nut Frosting

*I*n the 1960s, cream cheese frosting became wildly popular on carrot cake, almost a dessert emblem of the flower children's generation. They have long since grown up, but cream cheese frosting is as fresh and good as ever. Here, the cream cheese is mixed with dates and nuts to make a sort of creamy variation of old-fashioned date-nut bread. The frosting is still lovely on carrot cake, or gingerbread, or pound cake, or any number of cakes. It's even good on toast.

8 ounces cream cheese at room
   temperature
½ cup unsalted butter at room
   temperature
4 cups confectioners' sugar

1½ teaspoons pure vanilla extract
4 tablespoons chopped dates
4 tablespoons chopped pecans, walnuts
   optional: raisins or crystallized ginger
small pinch of salt

1. Cream the cheese and butter together until the mixture is smooth. Gradually add the sugar. Add the vanilla, continuing to beat. Finally, add the dates, nuts (and raisins or ginger, if using) and salt. If the frosting is too thick, add a bit of milk or cream, a teaspoon at a time. If it's too thin, add more sugar very gradually. After frosting the cake, refrigerate until serving, especially in warm weather.

Yield: frosting
to cover an
8-inch cake

Adapted from "Be
an Artist at the
Gas Range"

The Mystery Chef
and Your Gas
Company, 1935

Sour Cream Frosting

I had a friend who thought there were very few things in this world that would not be improved by a tablespoon of sour cream. I agree. Sour cream is not too far away from French crème fraîche. A quick approximation can be made by mixing sour and sweet cream. The classic recipe for making crème fraîche (when you are not in France and can't get the real thing) calls for adding a bit of buttermilk to sweet cream and letting it stand. This works, but it's very slow, while mixing sweet and sour cream is instant. Crème fraîche, like sour cream, is one of many bacterial gifts to the world, offsetting the bacterial curses as good fairies counter the bad. The tang of sour cream in frosting is a nice balance to the deep sweetness of confectioners' sugar.

Decorate Your Own Cakes
By Alice Bradley
Editor, Cooking Department
WOMAN'S HOME COMPANION
Copyright 1926

4 tablespoons unsalted butter	½ teaspoon pure vanilla extract
2 cups confectioners' sugar	small pinch of salt
4 tablespoons sour cream	

1. Cream the butter until it's light. Gradually add the sugar. When the mixture is smooth, add the sour cream, vanilla, and salt, and beat well.

Note: The frosting can be decorated with grated orange or lime zest scattered over the top, both as decoration and as flavoring.

Variation: You can easily make coconut frosting by adding shredded coconut to this recipe, and patting more coconut onto the sides of the frosted cake.

Yield: frosting to cover an 8-inch cake

Adapted from "Almanac and Cook Book"
Rumford Chemical Works, 1884

Chocolate Buttercream Frosting

The story of Hershey's chocolate is a saga of hard work and determination. The story of Baker Chocolate is a love story, an especially sweet chocolate tale. According to this Baker pamphlet, there was Prince Ditrichstein, a "brilliant young Austrian nobleman," and there was a waitress in a Viennese chocolate shop, Babette Baldauf, "daughter of an impoverished knight." One frosty afternoon in 1760, the Prince ventured into the shop to try the new drink from Central America that everyone was talking about: hot chocolate. What he found was the prettiest girl in all Vienna. Every day, he came back to drink hot chocolate and enjoy Babette's demure glances. "He completely forgets that a Prince may not look at a waitress . . . ." As a wedding gift, he commissioned a painting of his beloved in her waitressing dress. I don't know whether they lived happily ever after, but the portrait was displayed for many years in the Dresden Museum, and its replica, "La Belle Chocolatierre," became the Baker Chocolate logo. It can still be seen on cans of Walter Baker's Breakfast Cocoa.

1½ squares (1½ ounces) unsweetened chocolate

4 tablespoons unsalted butter

2 cups confectioners' sugar

¾ teaspoon pure vanilla extract

4 teaspoons milk or cream, or as needed

1. In a small saucepan over very low heat, melt the chocolate. Cool slightly.
2. Cream the butter until it's smooth and light; gradually add one cup of the sugar, continuing to beat. Add the vanilla and the melted chocolate. Beat well. Add the remaining sugar, beating well. Add the milk gradually, adding more if needed to reach the consistency for spreading.

Variations: *Orange Butter Frosting:* Omit the chocolate, vanilla, and milk. Instead, add the grated zest of one orange, ½ teaspoon orange extract, and 3 tablespoons orange juice. *Coffee Butter Frosting:* Omit the chocolate and milk. Instead, add ½ teaspoon cocoa and 3 to 4 tablespoons strong coffee. *Mocha Butter Frosting:* Omit the milk and instead add the same quantity of strong coffee.

Yield: frosting to cover an 8-inch cake

Adapted from "Best Chocolate Recipes"
Walter Baker & Company, Inc., 1932

Chocolate Sauce

I love vanilla ice cream, and I don't often see any point in covering it with anything. Why lose the pure, clean, cold, sweet dairy taste of vanilla and cream? But chocolate sauce over vanilla ice cream is an entirely different proposition. When the chocolate sauce is hot and the ice cream begins to melt under it, they merge into a luscious chocolatey cream. When the chocolate sauce is cold, the pleasures are separate. Together, the combination is reminiscent of such a simple joy as chocolate milk, all grown up now and turned into frozen cream. What bliss it all is, to have such choices!

3 squares (3 ounces) unsweetened chocolate
1/2 cup milk
3/4 cup sugar

1 tablespoon unsalted butter
pinch of salt
3/4 teaspoon pure vanilla extract

1. Melt the chocolate with the milk in a small saucepan over very low heat, stirring occasionally, until the chocolate is completely melted and the mixture is very smooth. Add the sugar and continue to cook until it's dissolved; add the butter and salt and cook for 3 to 5 minutes longer, until slightly thickened.

2. Remove from the heat. Let cool slightly and stir in the vanilla. Serve hot or cold.

Note: The sauce thickens as it stands, and becomes almost solid when it's refrigerated. It can be thinned with milk or cream. If you need to reheat it, either use a double boiler or heat it gently over low heat. In addition to ice cream, chocolate sauce can adorn a variety of desserts: cakes and some fruits and berries. Try it with strawberries, for instance — they're especially good with chocolate sauce.

Yield: 1½ cups

Adapted from "New Ways with Ice Cream"
Sealtest, Inc., 1949

Strawberry Sauce

"**D**oubtless God could have made a better berry," William Butler wrote, "but doubtless God never did." This is the famous quote about strawberries, and it's not far off the mark, depending on your taste for raspberries and blueberries. Once, we had to wait until spring to eat strawberries. They were all the more precious because they were seasonal. Now, they're available year-round in stores, frozen or shipped fresh from other regions. Strawberry sauce stretches their goodness, and makes a variety of other things happy, from ice cream to cheesecake to other berries.

1 quart strawberries, hulled and rinsed (see note)
1 cup sugar
optional: lemon juice (see note)

1. Place the strawberries in a bowl, pour the sugar over them, mix very gently and let stand for 1 hour.
2. Mash the strawberries lightly.
3. Put the berries into a saucepan over low heat, and cook gently just until they reach the boiling point. Remove from the heat. Serve hot or cold.

Note: The original recipe indicates that blackberry, raspberry, or peach sauce may be prepared using the same method. With any of these fruits, including strawberries, a few drops of lemon juice before or after cooking helps to accent the flavor. Note too that there isn't anybody who could tell you that these strawberries aren't perfectly delicious *without* being cooked, especially with a little cream or yogurt or sour cream.

Yield: about 4 cups

Adapted from "Davis Cook Book"
Davis Baking Powder, c. 1905

Whipped Cream Sauces

*I*s it possible to grow tired of whipped cream? No. But, just for a change, on a quiet day, there are other things that can be done with a cup of heavy cream. It depends on your mood, the state of your pantry, and what will be going under the cream. But whatever you do with it, whipped cream is always there for you.

Chocolate Whipped Cream

Whip 1 cup heavy cream until soft peaks form. Add 2 tablespoons chocolate syrup and whip until stiff.

Adapted from "Fifty-five Recipes"
Hershey Chocolate Corporation, undated

Cinnamon Whipped Cream

Lovely with baked apples.

Whip ¾ cup heavy cream until soft peaks form. Add 1½ tablespoons powdered sugar and ¾ teaspoon cinnamon. Whip until stiff.

Adapted from "The Sealtest Food
Adviser"
Sealtest, Inc., 1939

Chocolate Walnut Cream

Good with cake.

Heat 1 square (1 ounce) unsweetened chocolate and ¾ cup milk in the top of a double boiler and beat until thoroughly combined. In a separate bowl, combine 6 tablespoons sugar, 2 tablespoons cake flour, and a pinch of salt, and gradually add this mixture to the chocolate. Cook until thickened, stirring constantly. Cook 5 minutes longer, stirring occasionally. Add 1 tablespoon butter, cool slightly, and add 1 teaspoon vanilla. Chill. Whip 1 cup heavy cream. Fold the whipped cream and ½ cup chopped walnuts into the chocolate sauce.

Adapted from "Cake Secrets"
Swans Down Cake Flour, 1941

Coffee Whipped Cream

This is as good as the coffee you make it with, and at its best, it is absolutely delicious. Using gelatin results in whipped cream that will hold its shape, even in warm weather. Excellent with chocolate ice cream or cake.

Sprinkle ½ teaspoon gelatin over 2 tablespoons strong coffee in a cup. Let stand 5 minutes. Place the cup in a pan of very hot water and stir the gelatin until it dissolves. Whip 1 cup heavy cream with 2 tablespoons sugar and ¼ teaspoon pure vanilla extract until soft peaks form. Add the gelatin mixture and 2 additional tablespoons coffee and whip until stiff.

Adapted from "Coffee or Tea?"
Maxwell House, undated, c. 1920

Art Credits

"Bananas in the Modern Manner," Banana Growers Association, New York, NY. 1930. 14, 15.

"Bananas Take a Bow," Meloripe Fruit Company, Boston, MA. Undated. 8.

"Birds Eye Cook Book," Frosted Foods Sales Corp. 1941. 10.

"Borden's Eagle Brand Book of Recipes," The Borden Company, NY. Undated.Title, 49, 78, 88.

"Borden's Evaporated Milk Book of Recipes," The Borden Company, NY. Undated. Cover, 9, 56.

"Cake Secrets," Igleheart Bros. 1919. Cover (three), 13.

"Cake Secrets," Igleheart Brothers, Inc., Evansville, IN. 1928. 22, 25.

"The Calumet Baking Book," Calumet Baking Powder Co. 1931. Jacket, Cover, 13, 81 (three).

"Calumet Cook Book," Calumet Baking Powder Co., Chicago, IL. Undated. Cover.

"Ceresota Cook Book," The Northwestern Consolidated Milling Co., Minneapolis, MN. Undated. Cover (two).

"Cheese and Ways to Serve It," Kraft-Phenix Cheese Corporation, Chicago, Il. 1931. 20.

"Choice Recipes " Walter Baker & Co., Ltd. Dorchester, MA. 1901. Title page.

"Choice Recipes," Walter Baker & Co., Ltd., Dorchester, MA. 1916. 84.

"Cocoa and Chocolate," Walter Baker & Co., Ltd., Dorchester, MA. 1917. 39.

"Condensed Milk," NY Condensed Milk, New York, NY. 1887. 86.

"A Cookery Expert's New Recipes," Hershey Chocolate Company, Hershey, PA. Undated. 36.

"The Cream Top Book of Tested Recipes," Cream Top Bottle Corporation, Albany, NY. Undated. 55.

"Dainty Desserts for Dainty People," Charles B. Knox, Johnstown, NY. 1901. 3 (two), 44.

"Decorate Your Own Cakes," Woman's Home Companion, 1926. 83.

"Delightful Cooking," Corn Products Refining Co., New York, NY. Undated. 44.

"Del Monte Fruit Book," California Packing Corporation, San Francisco, CA. 1926. 8.

"Discovered," The Club Aluminum Company, Chicago, IL. Undated. 64.

"Douglas Oil for Best Salads and Better Cooking," Douglas Company, Cedar Rapids, IA. 1918. 53.

"Downright Delicious," Sun-Maid Raisin Growers, Fresno, CA. Undated. Cover, 24.

"Electric Cookery by Hotpoint," Edison General Electric Appliance Co., Inc., Chicago, IL. Undated. 48, 60.

"Favorite Recipes of the Movie Stars," Tower Books, New York, NY. 1931. 54.

"Frigidaire Recipes," Frigidaire Corporation, Dayton, OH. 1929. 6, 63.

"Food Surprises," The Mirro Test Kitchen. Undated. Jacket, 47 (two), 72.

"Getting the Most out of Foods," Corning Glass Works, Corning, NY. Undated. 30.

"Gold Medal Flour Cook Book," Washburn-Crosby Co., Minneapolis, MN. 1910. 43.

"Good Pies," Merrell-Soule Company, Syracuse, NY. Undated. 40, 42.

"Healthful Living," Battle Creek Food Company, Battle Creek, MI. Undated. 10.

"Henry's Cook Book and Household Companion," John E. Henry & Co., New York, NY. Jacket.

"Hershey's Recipes" Hershey Chocolate Corporation, Hershey, PA. Cover, Borders, 12, 38.

"Home Baked Delicacies," Igleheart Brothers, Evansville, IN. 1929. 85.

"Hotpoint Electric Cooking and Home Canning Book," Edison General Electric Appliance Company, Inc., Chicago, IL. Undated. Jacket (spine), 16, 46, 76.

"The Housewive's Almanac," Kellogg Company, Battle Creek, MI. 1938. 68.

"How to Make Tempting Nutritious Desserts," Hansen's Laboratory, Inc., Little Falls, NY. 1941. 4.

"Jell-O, America's Most Famous Dessert," The Genesee Pure Food Co., Le Roy, NY. Undated. 62

"The Jell-O Girl Entertains," The Jell-O Company, Inc., Le Roy, NY. Undated. Cover (two).

"Jell-O, Quick Easy Wonder Dishes," The Jell-O Company, Inc., Le Roy, NY. Undated. 5, 57.

"The Latest Cake Secrets," General Foods Corporation, New York, NY. 1934. 21, 75, 80.

"Lilly of the Valley," Winters & Prophet Canning Co., Rochester, NY.1925. 69.

"Maxwell House: Coffee or Tea?" Cheek-Neal Coffee Co. Undated. 31.

"Menu Magic in a Nutshell," California Walnut Growers Association, Los Angeles, CA. Cover.

"Monarch Cook Book," Malleable Iron Range Co., Beaver Damn, WI. 6.

"Nabisco," National Biscuit Company. Undated. 2.

"New Magic in the Kitchen," The Borden Company, New York, NY. Undated. 70.

"New Party Cakes," General Mills, Inc., Minneapolis, MN. 1931. 19.

"New Perfection Cook Book," The Cleveland Foundry Co. 1912. 5.

"Original Menus," Curtice Brothers Co., Rochester, NY. 1908. Title, Contents, 7.

"Proven Recipes," Corn Products Refining Co., New York, NY. 17.

"Pyrex Experts Book on Better Cooking," Corning Glass Works, Corning, NY. 1924. Cover.

"Recipe and Instruction Book," Hamilton Beach Mixette, Racine,WI. Cover, 33.

"Reliable Recipes and Helpful Hints," Calumet Baking Powder, Chicago, IL. Undated. 28.

"Royal Baker and Pastry Cook," Royal Baking Powder Co., New York, NY. Undated. 45, 52.

"Royal Desserts Recipes," Standard Brands Incorporated, 1940. 11.

"Rumford Fruit Cook Book," Rumford Company, Providence, RI, 1927. Cover (two), 29, 58, 71.

"The School Lunch," Postum Co, Inc., New York, NY. 1928. 35.

"Secrets of Coffee Flavor," Cheek-Neal Coffee Company, 1927. 65.

"The Silent Servant," B.T.H. Electric Refrigerator, Undated. 59, 67.

"Sunkist Orange Recipes," California Fruit Growers Exchange, Los Angeles, CA, 1940. Cover, 34.

"Super Chief Cook Book," Santa Fe Lines, Undated. 23.

"Unusual Recipes," Borden's Condensed Milk Company, New York, NY, 1911. 66.

"Washington Flour," Wilkins-Rogers Milling Co., Washington D.C., Undated. 26.

"WFBL Cook Book of the Stars," Onondaga Radio Broadcasting Corp., Syracuse, NY, 1945. 74.

"What Shall I Cook Today?," Lever Brothers Company, Cambridge, MA, Undated. 79.

"A Year of Recipes," Abbott Dairies, Inc. 1933. 61.

"Your Share," General Mills, 1943. 77.

Bibliography

Ayto, John, *The Diner's Dictionary; Food and Drink from A to Z.* Oxford University Press, 1993.

Bloom , Carole, *The International Dictionary of Desserts, Pastries, and Confections.* Hearst Books, 1995.

Claiborne, Craig, *The New York Times Food Encyclopedia.* Times Books, 1985.

Cowan, Ruth Schwartz, *More Work for Mother: The Ironies of Household Technology from the Open Hearth to the Microwave.* Basic Books, Inc., 1983.

Jones, Evan, *American Food: The Gastronomic Story.* E. P. Dutton, 1975.

Levenstein, Harvey, *Revolution at the Table.* Oxford University Press, 1988.

Mariani, John F., *The Dictionary of American Food.* Hearst Books, 1994.

Plante, Ellen M., *The American Kitchen 1700 to the Present: From Hearth to Highrise.* Facts on File, 1995.

Shapiro, Laura, *Perfection Salad: Women and Cooking at the Turn of the Century.* Farrar, Straus and Giroux, 1986

Trager, James, *The Enriched Fortified Concentrated Country-Fresh Lip-Smacking Finger-Licking International Unexpurgated Foodbook.* Grossman Publishers, 1970.

Trager, James, *The Food Chronology.* Henry Holt, 1995.

Index